POETRY MY ARSE

POETRY my arse

A POEM BY

BRENDAN KENNELLY

BLOODAXE BOOKS

ISBN: 1 85224 322 8 hardback edition
         1 85224 323 6 paperback edition

First published 1995 by
Bloodaxe Books Ltd, 20\9\95
P.O. Box 1SN,
Newcastle upon Tyne NE99 1SN.

Bloodaxe Books Ltd acknowledges
the financial assistance of Northern Arts.

Cover printing by J. Thomson Colour Printers Ltd, Glasgow.

Printed in Great Britain by
Bell & Bain Limited, Glasgow, Scotland.

in memory of
MARK STURM
COLIN O'DONOVAN
DICK O'BRIEN

ACKNOWLEDGEMENTS

Thanks are due to Ralph Steadman, for the cover picture of Kanooce, and to Martin Honeysett for his frontispiece drawing of a Liffey rat, which was first published (as 'Depravo the Rat') in *Bert Fegg's Nasty Book for Boys and Girls* (Eyre Methuen, 1974). I would also like to thank Louise Kidney for her help in typing this book.

Publisher's note: That's enough arse-licking! We have deleted the rest of Brendan Kennelly's acknowledgements, including a note of thanks to his editor which was too brown-tongued to print here.

POETRY MY ARSE

1 *Through the eyes of a prim little prick, much of the time*

3 *Holy Mary, mother of God, plant a laugh in this poor sod*

ACENOTE

This poem concerns a poet, poetry, language and various forms of relationship. The poet, Ace de Horner, moves through his poetry, the city, different relationships. He broods a lot. He broods on words, people, streets, dreams, the Liffey, Janey Mary, his self. And he broods in such a way or ways that terms such as poem, novel, story, drama or play merge with each other to form an Acenote which he often finds very odd. His brooding estranges whatever he broods on. The poem he writes may not be the poem he wished to write or even the poem he believes he has written. His own concoctions (he will not call them creations) are frequently bizarre to himself. Am I really guilty o' that? He seems to wish to control what laughs at the notion of being controlled.

Ace de Horner moves through Dublin, a post-colonial city. She is not Irish. She is not English. What marks a post-colonial city? I feel a bit lost trying to answer that one. In fact, I'd say that this feeling a bit lost in history and language is probably the first mark of post-colonialism. A bit lost. So let's pretend to be bloody well certain. Pretence. This pretence helps to explain the second mark: the fact that caricature, the art of spontaneous, amusing and instructive distortion, is a way of life and a constant mode of expression. Let's twist again. This poem adopts caricature as an essential part of its method; it is compelled to become a conscious victim of what it tries to explore. One cannot escape the consequences of colonialism; one must turn the results of political imposition and manipulation into a number of artistic devices which are, in turn, at odds with each other, thereby continuing to reflect the conflicting nature of the original political/military situation. The poem, therefore, is necessarily a labyrinth of comic distortion of everything one is, feels, says, writes and dreams of putting forward as "serious". *Sure you might be gettin' above yourself or losin' the run o' yourself. The run o' yourself* involves not being too keen to escape the charming, menacing shadows of the comic labyrinth. *You had a master once. You were a slave once.* (No, I wasn't, you eejit). *Don't ever forget that, son.* (Why should I bother to forget what I can't begin to remember?). *Never forget it, son, and you'll be fine, you'll be fine in no time at all. No time at all.*

The third consequence of post-colonialism is incest, a special kind of unavoidable social and cultural incest. Up against it, that's what we are. No escape. Up against it. And up against each other. Dublin is a helplessly (one is tempted to say happily) incestuous city where we feed off each other's characters, marriage troubles, drink problems, money messes, sex cavortings, job catastrophes and other attractive forms of misfortune, distress, failure and crack. If you don't like implacable gossip, stay out of Dublin. If you do, you're in heaven. Or hell. Pray tell. *Pure joy, me oul' flower, pure joy.*

The pure savagery of gossip is stimulating. It shows a dynamic interest in other people's affairs and is most often accompanied by an equally dynamic resolution not to know oneself. For the crime being, anyway. To this extent, an accomplished gossip is a venomous altruist or, at his or her "best", an un-bridled comic satanist of the tongue. Dubliners love this gossipycomicsatanism. It would be a shame not to do justice to this. *Ace de Horner at your service, sir, madam. Are you with me, Kanooce? O isn't that the ugliest calamity of a dog you ever saw in your natural?*

Gossip has many features in common with poetry. They are both born of hunger; mental, emotional, intellectual, physical hunger of various kinds. They both, when they are "good", have a special kind of energy, a kick, that's pretty hard to equal almost anywhere else. They are both predatory; gossip preys on other people's problems, failures, even tragedies; poetry feeds on feelings, both the feelings of the poet and, frequently, the feelings of other people as picked up and used by the poet. And both the gossip and the poet enjoy a certain detachment, often a safe detachment, a protected perspective that enables them to dispense their individual versions of local lies and cosmic truths with a perfectly desireable blend of passion and style. Style, above all. Style is the man or the woman. How you say it is how it is. Why you say it need never be known. The protected perspective is often cherished by those who seem to believe they are laying themselves on the line. This very fact contains within its depths the fertile, bristling seed of the caricature of itself. Is there any developed style that doesn't? Can there be any real conviction in poetry without an accompanying, deeply threaded self-mockery? Will not your "truth" always show a disturbing tendency to dance with your "lies"? This is the dance of caricature. It is a smiling, searing, accusing, revealing dance.

In a culture where the impulse to caricature is so widespread, "normal" and strong, its influence naturally and inevitably spreads into language, emotions, attitudes to tolerance and justice and what passes for ideas. On the whole, anecdotes and yarns replace ideas. Can anecdotes, stories become adequate substitutes for an inherited or personally achieved philosophy in poetry? This poem tries to grapple with that problem. Most English poets, even when they don't study their philosophers, are nearly always aware of them, directly or indirectly. Irish poets have little or no such available support. But what am I saying? *Didja hear this man? It'll give ya a right bloody giggle. Ya know yar man screwin' yar woman in Trinity College? Well Jaysus let me tell ya...*

The fourth consequence of post-colonialism is vitality – that unique (is it freakish?) vitality derived from feeling a bit lost, caricatured, and being the incestuous victim-propagator of gossip. How, one may ask, can vitality emanate from such activities and conditions? A primary reason is that such conditions and activities guarantee and sustain a certain isolation or loneliness, often wearing a mask of boisterousness, in what is probably the most garrulous city in Christendom. This, I think, is what Brendan Behan meant when he said that Dublin offers a lot of loneliness but little or no solitude. In loneliness we are severed; in solitude we may grow strong. Loneliness, given the opportunity, preys on others. Solitude tends to explore the self. A severed emotional predator is an energetic animal (though this predatory energy is, I believe, what James Joyce had in mind when he referred to Dublin as the centre of the paralysis of the universe). How can energy be equated with paralysis? Because it is not interested in *relating* to what it singles out for attention but is very interested in *exploiting* it. *Poetry My Arse* tries to explore this ruthless energy of exploitation in different ways and at different levels. I am especially interested in the nature of the strength and vitality springing from the deliberate rejection of the vulnerability and potential of open, complex relationship. And this poem asks: does poetry fuck poets up? Or does it liberate/educate/enlighten them in the area of human relationships? Has poetry a destructive power we refuse to acknowledge? And is that destructive power all the more fierce when rooted in a genuine, constant verbal energy? Dublin's verbal energy is damned delightful. Wilde, Yeats, O'Casey, Flann O'Brien, Sam Beckett, Brendan Behan, Roddy Doyle and others have all relished this. Yesterday morning, on a train, a man from Skerries (that's where they ate Saint Patrick's goat and the Saint cursed the Skerries folk, condemning them to bleat creepy goatgossip forever) asked me if I'd heard of the Kerry cowboy. I said no. He said 'His balls were black from ridin' the range. It was an old-fashioned Stanley range.' Then the joke-dam burst and flowed. The train enjoyed it, it gave a couple of appreciative hops. A retired Civil Servant pitched in with a few jewel-jokes of his own. Dubliners don't just speak English, their own brand of it, they wear it *'like me favourite gear'*. They show off in it, preen and strut in it, take their holidays in it, go to town in it, wave it like a football flag. *And how's your belly for spots, darlin'? Same as yours for pimples, love.* This is all fair enough. Language shouldn't just be an instrument of so-called rational and/or irrational communication. It should be aired, steered through pollution, allowed to swallow pubsmoke, trawl through Internet, swoon through Rave parties, flee through E, be dipped in the cancery Sellafield sea, (should all these Dublin Bay prawns be hospitalised?) , persuaded to sniff its way through graffiti-slashed Ladies and Gents, hauled in and out through traffic, compete with cursing drivers, squat with beggars in reasonably charitable sunlight, be introduced to brothe-lisers making speeches, ripple like baby demons through talk-to-me-dirty and the perfectly chaste gasps of lovers in bed, at bus-stops, on chapel steps and down all the sweet, stinking days and laneways of the second city of Empire, Dublin.

To try to do justice to this second-city-Empire language, Ace de Horner becomes a kind of shuffling arena of voices. Somewhere along the journey, my own voice steps into this poem simply because it must, it passionately wants to be heard by Ace, by Janey Mary, by all the other voices, by the reader. Then, very quickly, Ace de Horner takes over again. Takes over what? Takes over the fact that he was taken over. So he throws me out and takes himself over again. In the post-colonial situation, the question of identity is paramount and apparently permanent. The resolutely thoughtless hang on with unquestioning and fierce "patriotic" fidelity to what they consider to be their identity; the thoughtful question it incessantly, in the language available to them. Any confrontation of identity involves a deliberate act of listening to different internal and external voices. One must be calmly attentive in Babel. So, in this poem, the different voices erupt, clash, mingle, disentangle themselves, go their own lonely roads, lonely streets and riverways, setting up, as they journey on through loss and discovery and conferences on redemption, a voiceline or voicenet or voicelink in which may be heard echo-parodies of what has been said earlier, caricatures of sincere moments, distortions of attempts to be emotionally and intellectually serious *(for God's sake how can anyone be serious with a bollocks like that runnin' the show?)*, a world of voices that is at one moment an intricate flash of knives in sunlight *(is this a picnic?)* and the next a love-duet so ardent and intense it simply cannot be taken seriously because *'one o' them is bound to cop on to the other before the year is out, know what I mean, like?'*

In Dublin, the joke is king because the reality of any person, event or achievement can be measured by the extent to which he or she or it is parodied, twisted and caricatured. That is why a genuine word of praise, when uttered and heard, is so unutterably beautiful. That is also why Dublin is one of the funniest cities in the world. The range of laughter is as wide as the events, people, anecdotes, encounters, pictures, thoughts and expressions that inspire it, going from subtle mindplay to endlessly repeated obvious jokes. Jokes are as thick and tasty in the air as various forms of pollution. A joke, said Nietzsche, is an epitaph for an emotion. By this definition, Dublin is a graveyard of feelings. And the jokes are non-stop, well timed, accurate, hilarious, shapely, spikey, often deadly. Any extended poem about Dublin must involve this joke-making genius. Needless to say, this poem itself will become a joke. Joke begets joke begets joke, let's be serious about that. The trick is to continue to parody the parody, caricature the caricature, cartoon the cartoon. That ring around the moon is a ring o' giggles made of Irish jokes, Jewish jokes, Kerryman jokes, English jokes, women jokes, gay jokes, AIDS jokes, jokes about the latest politician-in-a-brothel, jokes about the latest scandal of whatever kind. From Nietzsche's standpoint, Dublin must be one of the funniest graveyards on earth, full of comic corpses *bustin' their coffins laughin'*.

Yet I believe there is a remote, lonely corner of the mind, out of reach of incest or Dublincest, that no amount of parody and caricature can twist or disfigure or render ridiculous. I've tried to let Ace de Horner discover and live these moments. Unshareable, private, lonely moments. But real. More real that the loud, ubiquitous disfigurings. But there's many a mouth will say 'They're only caricatures too.' Many a mouth including, at times, my own.

Is language now so flogged and bludgeoned by all of us, by writers, critics, journalists, politicians, speech-makers, speech-writers, lecturers, cause-promoters, diplomats, interviewers, interviewees, Government information spokespeople, reviewers, lawyers, judges, pro-abortionists, pro-lifers, business men and women, computer disciples, terrorists, terrorists-turned-politicians and theory-besotted academics that the act of trying to write a poem necessarily brings one into contact with apparently universal linguistic perversions (which one shares and propagates) granted sophisticated status by sufficient numbers of practitioners who agree among themselves that this is the way to speak, this is the way to write, this is how we must strengthen our own position as we instruct and enlighten the public, the young, this is the point of aspiration, this is tellyspeak, radiospeak, videospeak, newspaperspeak, magazinespeak? Therefore, is it poemspeak also? Therefore, can a poem begin to be truthful (charming old word) without being infected? Should it? Can it? And is the joke-pulse beating endlessly, vigorously, scathingly, in all this 'culture' of infected witness?

There's some connection between Dublin's increasing violence and the kinds and uses of language I've mentioned. Mugging is now a popular pastime with youngsters in the city. I've been mugged myself and what I remember most about my blazingblue-eyed assailant is his language, a frenzied-deliberate repetition of two sentences before he, as they say, set upon me: *'Whatthefuckyalookinat? Whatthefuckyalookingat? Whatthefuckyalookinat?'* and *'Gimmeyarmoney! Gimmeyarmoney! Gimmeyarmoney!'* These two sentences were well rehearsed and impeccably delivered. I thought the repetition was particularly impressive. Hypnotically so, as it can sometimes be in poetry. Timor mortis conturbat me. I am sick, I must die. Lord, have mercy on me. Hypnotically effective, if repeated with sufficient intensity and precision. Memorable. Just like the kicks and punches. Fair dues to my mugger, however, he spared me the knife. Black handle. Are there unwritten poems waiting to mug writer and reader? Does imagination have something in common with muggers? A rehearsed violence waiting to explode? Does language spawn violence or violence beget language? I don't know. But I've tried to present both in this poem while knowing I don't know which is the origin of which.

Ace de Horner has a complex relationship with Dublin, its people, its language, its violence, its comic incest. He is, I think, caught between being a concerned coward and a genuine proponent of semi-throttled goodwill. One irony of city living is that, even in an expressive city like Dublin, a person usually cannot take part or intrude where he feels he should. (An American once said to me when I told her of an impending visit to New York, 'Make sure you don't look into the eyes of people in the streets'). Instead of going out into action, the city-walker goes into his own mind and follows the action there. Ace de Horner walks the streets and stalks himself. He is a loner obsessed with relationship. What is it? In personal terms? Is he capable of it? Or is he a freakish brooder on what he is condemned never to know fully? Never to know even partly, perhaps? Is he a kind of nobody? If so, what does the voice of a kind of nobody sound like? To himself? To another man? To a woman? To a dog? Is it God's mercy that we never completely know what our own voices sound like? If so, is it better to be a kind of nobody than somebody condemned to know what he really sounds like? There are certain kinds of ignorance for which one should be eternally grateful. Distance not only makes the heart grow fonder; it makes the voice grow tolerable.

There were times I believed, during the writing of this poem, that the real poet was, increasingly, Janey Mary, the person who is perhaps most impatient with poetry, with the poetry world. She works, connects, speaks, quips out of an accepted sense of her own reality. Poetry is imitation, Aristotle said. Imitation. Not the real thing. I've know Dublinwomen who were, who are so real, so genuine, so utterly there, in my presence, hilariously so, hurtfully so, that I wanted to have their voices heard. Poetry my arse. Indeed. It is not imitation. Was Aristotle on the bottle when he said it was? And poetry is not emotion recollected in tranquillity either. Not any more, it isn't. It's more like moments of terrifying clarity recollected in, and challenging, a state of habitual pressure, stress, even confusion. Poetry now is frequently a fugitive art, written by people on the run from stressful "responsibility". How can that be "imitation", of all things? You may deliberately, against all your so-called 'better judgment', give your life to poetry, yet if poetry emerges at all it does so with an arbitrary, wanton air that simply refuses to be dubbed reliable or responsible. It will never be taken for granted. It would be phoney, perhaps obscene, to think that it might be.

How much fakery glitters in the poetry world? How much pretentiousness, vanity, manipulation? A fair amount, I'd say, going by what I see when I take a peek into my own little heart. But is there anything that is not a theme? Anything that cannot be fed into the voiceline? A poet is not merely ninety-five per cent water (or thereabouts, give or take a few pints), daft as a high tide wired to a full moon. He is also, potentially, an interesting lump of raw material to himself, comparable to a crow's nest or a fire-alarm on the wall of a house, especially if he realises that his 'best moments' contain within themselves the mocking seed of their own caricatures. Even moments of life-changing passion can be a bit of a laugh, in retrospect. Even retrospect, in retrospect, can mock itself more convincingly.

But I go back to that 'remote, lonely corner of the mind' or soul, if I may use that word which means, to some people, something at once unproveable and undeniable. It is this remote, lonely corner that the poem struggles to get near, even, at certain brazen moments, to enter, to look around, to scrutinise, to celebrate. This place, this corner, this out-of-the-way spot in himself is where, I think, Ace de Horner is also trying to go. And the blinder he becomes the more clearly he sees it. Or so he believes. This, for me, is the source of his loneliness. And his loneliness is the source of whatever strength he has. Janey Mary is a travelling companion. The real poet? Would she make Aristotle change his mind? Pitbull Kanooce is a travelling companion. Kanooce is not an imitation of anything. But he's very good for poetry. Poetry is imitation, the dogma goes. If Kanooce knew that, he might eat it. So let the dog bite the dogma. *Just for the fun, like, just for the fun.* But the poem might bite him back, if it got half a chance. *Snap.* Real enough, if you felt it. How's that for imitation?

Loneliness and fun recognise each other, as do silence and expression, congestion and space, blindness and sight. *Poetry My Arse* moves among and through these states as it moves also through mental territories and the streets of Dublin, full of ghosts who were people and people who will be ghosts. On and on and on. It is a mindpoem and a streetpoem. I would hope, in the long run, that it's a kind of biting love-poem to a city where love, being rare, is all the more real when set against the unfailing flow of reductive, funny bitterness, the comic campaign against dignity that matters so much to so many. *And why not, me ould flower? Didja hear what yar man called his fuckin' book? Poetry My Arse, no less. Isn't it bloody gas? An' him a Trinity bleedin' College Professor! Trinity bleedin' College where they have no bleedin' knowledge! Poetry My Arse, my arse! Sure it's only a bag o' farts, if the truth was told...*

18

'If the truth was told.' I think we should stop using this word 'truth' in relation to poetry; when it is used, it usually flatters the poem, the poet, the reader, the critic. What is the 'truth' of Christ or Cromwell or Judas or Jack the Ripper or Saint Paul or Mick Mullally from Ringsend or my mesmeric little bugger of a Dublin mugger? 'Truth' is a word that is made to tell a lot of lies. I hope this poem demonstrates the manipulative humanity of those lies, those teeming, vigorous little fibs, in service to a 'truth' that cannot be fully articulated because it is ultimately silent or quietly disconnecting itself from inquiring minds or just moving away to another corner of the room or the world or itself. 'What is truth?' said jesting Pilate. The fascinating word there is 'jesting'. If we didn't mask our faces with smiles, our words with styles, our accounts of our dreams with a few useful distortions, our questions with some jesting disinclination to receive completely accurate answers, we'd hardly proceed to the next poem or bout of reading or appointment with friend or lover. I'm talking about a dance in which integrity steps it out with deception, honesty waltzes with a sneer and the light of one's mind trips the light fantastic with the shadow that cannot cease to haunt and activate the mind in ways that only darkness can. It seems logical that *Poetry My Arse* should seek to explore the blindness of poetry. Nothing is fixed, nothing is finished, the Liffey flows, the city roars, the phone rings, high in a tree a blackbird sings, a poem says something, a teeny-weeny something that is forgotten or twisted or loved or joked about or remembered in such a way it helps a woman staring at a grave in Wicklow to walk back home through three fields of agony, down a road of slightly lessening pain, up a laneway of small, sad relief, into a house where a few words help her to discover a 'truth' in herself which means now, this cold clear November day, she's prepared to stay alive and face it, thanks to the humane blindness of poetry.

BRENDAN KENNELLY

1

Through the eyes of a prim little prick, much of the time

The Song of Ace de Horner

I am the wind on the Liffey

I am the youngster fleeing the policeman on O'Connell Bridge

I am the Warrington Daycare Centre

I am the fire plan, the smoke alarm, the smoke that kills in seconds

I am the woman up from the country rambling among bargains,
fingering

I am the paperback written to lighten the journey

I am the newest rumour in the streets of Dublin, take
me to bed, spread me with the relish of prophecy, taste
me like a juicy honeymoon but above all add to me
add to me like a parody of the myth
you were born to hunger for

I am a thin tree trembling with growth like a leggy girl all promise

I am a terrified whisper on the phone

I am the scream that wakes me in the darkness

I am a crow's nest in a tree outside Manchester

I am your eyes seeing through me

I am the child's cry in the childminder's ear, where
on earth are my father and mother?

I am river canal sea street scandal pisstaker starving cat
graffiti Liffey rat white plastic bag in wild flight
over Dublin

I am a freezing midnight parking lot

I am gas, cheap gas, might explode

I am the jet's white line perfect in the raped sky

I am the Way Out

I am a guide bridge in a city hardly knowing
it is losing its heart

I am a BA (Hons) seeking Business in Europe

I am hailstones on the head of the red-haired
woman gaping at the train

I am half-way to anywhere

I am as apt a practitioner of pollution as any in
this particular country

I am short steps on a long journey

I am Lizzie in daylight wearing blue jeans white
shirt and caterpillar boots. Who now remembers
her shriek of delight in the butterfly night?

I am the lies of killers on television, in public places,
the obscene plausibility on their faces

I am nine silver birches displacing the Muses
th' other side o' Swords

I am blindness itself, I see the truth of that

I am the question I fear to answer

I am paper, things written on paper, paper drifting down
the Liffey to greet your eyes at ten past three next Sunday
afternoon. And tell me this, my Liffey stroller, are
you keeping the Sabbath holy or as near to holy
as makes no difference to any decent caricature of
love thy neighbour as thyself?

I am the rift in the family of poets, the hook in
the salmon's mouth

I am a tree split by lightning, a bird sings in
my stricken branches

I am Ace de Horner, who's that?

Old hat, darling, old hat, wisdom of a Liffey
rat, peace out of blood, truth out of lies, a
world glimpsed clearly by tired eyes that you
may find revealing though they open to grow blind

First words

'Mary, where are you? Mary! Mary O'Grady!'
– from the street, first words of Ace's morning.

Mary, where are you? Mary! Mary O'Grady!
Come here, sit down, have a coffee, save me from drowning.

Adam's apple

'I was raped,' she said
'by two youths who lay
on each other first on
the kitchen floor, then upped
and attacked me.'

'That's horrible,' he murmured
touching his Fellini shirt
at a point below his Adam's apple.

'It was hell,' she said.

'I know that,' he said, 'I know that.
I think I'd like to write
a poem about it,
a vivid poem that would be widely read.'

She looked at his finger
operating near his Adam's apple.

'Poetry my arse,' she said.

Who knows, Annie?

On her back, Annie Grant
stretches out in the sun in Queen Street.
The first tentative moments of summer
touch her like a shy young lover.
Who knows, Annie, who knows? This could be
the real thing before the year is over.

Overheard streetballad

The streets of Dublin
are my Parnassus,
I love to walk 'em
night and day.
If you don't like me
you can kiss my assus
and go rob your cousins
in Amerikay.

Plans

Moneytrouble Ace has plans to save
Staring at grass on a famine grave.
His eyes are drawn to a starving slave.
From end to end
   of this dump-the-young land
     he struggles to celebrate
       what he can't understand.

Shiver

Ace shivered.
I do not own my life,
nothing I am is mine,
he thought. The river
blackened in winter light,
it wasn't bad being nothing,
the shiver passed, Ace tightened
his scarf about his throat,
swallowed the icy night.

Waiting for a bus

'Why is there so much hatred in Ireland?'
the grey man asked Ace, waiting for a bus.
'Why is this place a hell of hatred?'
His words were neither sad nor ominous,

just casual. Nevertheless, they'd earned
the right to be uttered and heard.
Ace had no answer though his heart burned
to know. He knew nothing and had no word

to offer the man who'd lived seventy years
discovering a truth that hadn't made him bitter
but alert as a druggie in O'Connell Street
livingdying for the shot to zoom out of down here

and wing up there above the venomed lies,
the merciless yarns about everyone in hell.
'Why the hatred?' the grey man asked again.
The poet was dumb and stupid as usual,

he was a hole in a wall, a streetspit,
the failure a boy believes in enough to kill
himself, a slave who doesn't recognise
his slavery now, and never will

until the hole is filled in, the spit swept away,
the failure treated with the same scorn as success,
the slave set free in hope of loving his freedom
and the poet safely ensconced in his favourite bus.

Walking back from Croke Park
after the All-Ireland Football Final

'Fuckin' culchies! Fuckin' bogmen! Fuckin' shithouse walls!'

                                    In Lower Gardiner Street
stones of abuse hit the heads
of Donegal supporters
                    historical with victory over Dublin.
Then the real stones pelt in a shower,
men and women run, green and gold in flight.
Behind railings, the children, all power now,

bomb the culchies and bogmen,
and curse and swear and call to each other
to stone the bastards then set 'em on fire.

Ace stands in a doorway, looking on.
Nobody wonders who is that man
in the doorway, looking on.

The violence of children, he thinks, I haven't seen before.

The children run. The stones are at rest.
Curses lie like dead flies in the dust.
The city roars ahead as the city must.

Ace lingers, shoulder to the door
as if he'd stand calmly there forever
close to children, sport, murder,

voices of the future.

Cry

Ace has never heard a cry
like this in his life
in the cry-as-you-like city.

At three in the morning
the cry splits the trees
rustling and whispering

in his accommodating head.
It slices the heavy roads
into pieces and ices his blood.

Yet it passes, it passes.
And morning comes
through all the windows

hit by the cry several hours before.
Where has the cry gone?
Who uttered it? Why?

The questions vanish too,
forgotten like the dead, like people
out of work, like me, like you.

Only when Ace closes his eyes
in a dark room, only then
is the cry alive again

cutting the darkness into thin strips
his heart uses
to stitch his lips.

An icy star

Loneliness hit her like a fist.
Her heart staggered, recovered.
She turned down a sidestreet
half-noticing the child begging on the steps

of the half-ruined house. Then she saw
the child was shivering. She passed on.
She was being eaten now, not for the first time.
Something was here, something was gone

forever. If you told her she was being chewed
by a ravenous star, she'd have believed you
but you, like me, were somewhere else.

She was a cry midnighting through blood.
If all else was false, the cry was true.
It was her heart, her mind, her gut, her pulse.

She throbbed beyond the world a while, returned
to human streets, an icy star that burned,
burned her loneliness through

till she began, again, to try
to know what to do.

Happy

'She lied to me the night
                she met me.
I lied to her before
                and after she became my wife.
Two for joy, she lilted bright an' early
            and though she never
shared her gizzard truth with me
            nor I mine with her

        we had a happy life.'

Gist

She'd loved him (she told herself) for forty years
yet after he was gone
she couldn't remember a single sentence
he'd spoken in all that time.

       Forty years together.
       Not a sentence could she remember.

But she got the gist of the man,
the gist, and that was enough
to help her remember those crucial nights
she'd called his bluff

when he hunched into the kitchen
rain on his coat and hat
hands darting at nothing, despairing
eyes of a drowning rat.

Pram

On the Liffeybed a pram
lies like a broken marriage.
Not even the all-knowing Liffey
will ever know the full story.
       Overhead
gulls scream for bread,
for anything, this cold day.
Maggie MacDonagh begs on the bridge.
Thousands shiver homewards.
No one looks her way
but that won't stop Maggie
begging the air that doesn't give a damn,
her eyes deeper than the river
housing a broken pram.

The ravens

'By the time the ravens came I was old.
Time was the sun played like a pup in the heavens,
I was handy on the feet, I tricked and fooled
the loveliest women ever danced with men.

Fool talk I excelled at. That's the talk
they wanted and that's the guff I gave 'em.
I'd cycle anywhere, pitchdark or moonlight
so long as she opened her legs in a ditch.

They say women are bitches. No, men are fools
and I as big a fool as ever was left alone
in the end, an empty bed, my few acres sold
for drink, all right now, healthy enough, long miles
behind me, body withering, yes, withering bones.

There's hope, you say, good bit of the story left untold.
By the time the ravens came, I was old.'

Happy

'I like sleeping with Stephen.
I like sleeping with Stephen's daddy too.
Neither knows I sleep with the other.
I keep two men happy. And you?'

Enough!

Three angels stand guard
over the Bank of Ireland,
each one a distant lover

always there, not always seen
by Ace and his ilk
down-eyed about the town.

But once, late February,
an evening of ice and music
amid Scottish Rugby ecstasy

under a cool moon
in a ruthless blue sky
Ace saw the angels and he

stopped to stare as he had
rarely stared. Yes, yes,
the angels were there, there

against the blue ruthless sky
over the Bank of Ireland.
And suddenly men and women

were dancing to the icy music,
dancing under the angels
not always seen but always there

like love between men who kill
each other for reasons they'll never
understand

in this ghastly, ghostly, murderous, gossipy,
old, ecstatic land –
love will up and out and live

again
in the slaughtering hearts of men
heedless of icy music

this blue true-mooned February night
of angels guarding the dancers
in this ancient city of light.

If what he sees is true for a moment
it might be true forever. Ace
might ask the god of the river

if he needed to, but he
doesn't, he has witnessed the dancing,
glimpsed the love, sensed the sea,

stared at angels, stared
at angels till he shared the company
of those who dared

to fill the streets with heaven
the sky with hope
a moment in a city of love

a moment, enough, enough!

Cap

The old countryman, his back to the Bank of Ireland,
    head down, holds his cap out
        to the crowd passing,
            caring, uncaring.

Is he begging or sneering?

Industrial unrest

'They're playing Beethoven on RTE!
The strike is over!
Peace at last!

And God be praised, no more talk of blame!'

'What a shame!'

Way

Ace is a leaf in the river today.
The river flows him where it wills
until the riverway is the Aceleafway.

Dying fish

A mother and her child, gravely ill,
queue at a children's hospital in Lima.
As the child dies
fifteen fighter-jets
sicken the Peruvian skies
over the heads of girls
from Loreto College, Crumlin
offering a peace-carpet
(Brigid gives a sword to a beggarman:
'Exchange it for food')
to people of peace in the grounds of the Pentagon.
But the Pentagon refuses permission
'for security reasons'.
Ace goes down to the river
where dying fish increase, increase
and the poisoned deeps of Ireland
rejoice
at their own peace.

'We failed the mountains'

'The mountains have always been our friends.
They gave us snow and rain.
They gave the sun a chance to do all
in its power for us. It did.

We gave the mountains names
to do them justice. Touching heaven
is a mountain's justice.
We learned green and light and rock from them,
were educated by their ice.
They gave us dreams, more than we ever dared
to take, follow, be tested by. We couldn't handle their generosity.
They instructed us in kinship and difference
of waterfall and stream.
       We let ourselves down.
       We failed the mountains.
       They wanted to make us real
       but we'd rather be anonymous
victims of the ever-deepening All-American Scream.'

Starved

Starved Ace kneels at love's dark border
eating the hairy eye, the furry burger.

In and out

I slip in and out of myself
Ace slips in and out of himself
till he is me
and I am he.

Which of us was born with fire in the head,
fire in the heart and fire in the eyes?
Which of us fought with demons in gutterhouses
and grew to be at home with all kinds of cries?

Which of us learned speech of rain and wind
and went beyond the light into the speaking dream
that lay unnoticed in streets and quick laneways
designed, you'd swear, to contain a girl's scream?

Which of us stood and listened to the scream
and plucked it from the air to store it in his blood
flowing through stories growing in the mind
like briars and grasses on the side of the road?

Which is which, how is how, why is why,
slit the wrist, the flood will flow,
Ace slips in and out of himself, so do I,
that's all we know, or think we know.

The prize

Ace de Horner won Kanooce
in the only doglotto
ever held in Ireland.

Ace bought his ticket
in a shop in Merrion Square
and he took priceless care
over his numbers

3 6 9 18 27 39

He was sitting in a pub in Bluebell
when the numbers rolled out
like pearls from the telly.

Ace de Horner slid to the floor.

          He'd won it! He'd won it!
The only doglotto
ever held in Ireland!

Would your average greedy bastard
(such as me)
dare dream of more?

Next day, he collected Kanooce
from another shop in Merrion Square.

Jesus in heaven, did anyone ever cast eyes
on a creature
ugly as this?

Ace looked at Kanooce,
Kanooce stared at Ace
with perhaps the same thought in his head,
his lessthanbeautiful, pitbull head.

It'd frighten the dead!

But they got together,
they got together,
poet and dog
and walked along Merrion Square
(Willie Yeats lives there, the oul' star)
and they ambled through Dublin
sizing each other up
getting the feel of each other
knowing 'twas likely
they'd live together
for quite a little kingdom to come.

On they went, a clear-the-street pair,
on to the Bluebell cell.
Ace opened the door
Kanooce sniffed the air

looked at de Horner, the cell

and nosed in.

The lotto is over, thought Ace, the prize is won.
Now what is about to begin?

Main course

Fartface whiskeys, 'Listen, chum! If I'd my way
I'd cut the balls off every fucking queer.'
The hostess's terrified whisper reaches Ace,
'Careful, please! He controls my husband's career.'

A wee soul to save

'In this country,' old Sexton said,
'there's one thing ya have to learn,
one thing ya must do.
Ya must tell 'em to fuck off
when it's right to tell 'em to fuck off.
It's immoral not to.
Otherwise, they'll eat your soul,
d'ya hear me, eat your soul, my son.
Don't rot away in respectable silence
or turn the daylight into a grave.
Say it when ya must, not when ya can.
Ya have a wee soul to save.'

The cats and the book

The cats are clawing the book to pieces.
Black cat is a frantic knife having
the time of her life, hacking the hated pages.
Fat grey cat is going to war, blood
smeared all over her whiskers, she is
the Mother of Battles and every scar on her skin
pronounces infallible bulls. Brown cat
is spitting hate at every neighbour in
the enemyhood, she has brought forth
subversive kittens in an hour of labour.
Old white cat is cool and deadly,
a creature of few kisses, but no hiss misses
its target. This one has seen and killed it all
before, and will again, it's wine and roses
for her, it's the special continental plant,
the expensive surgical job on the nose,
the most avant-garde perfume in town,
the show that puts a stop to all the shows.
If even a scrap of a single page survives
the fierce assaults of fangs and claws
old white cat will see that nothing lives
apart from what is favoured by her bristling laws.

So it's the end of the line for the book
as we have known it, the cats will write
another book, we'll all read it, God send us luck
as we face each other in the purring light,
field mice trapped in the eyes of cats tonight.

Zany rain

'He started talking dirty to me on the phone.
I felt silly, trembling all over,
he talked like I'd never heard him talk before,
I was shaking, shaking, and then my God
I had this orgasm in that quiet office,
by myself, alone,
and as I came and came
his low sweet mocking laughter
fell all over me
like zany rain
on the dimpled river.'

Home

'My mother had the same name as myself.
Bernadette.
When I was fifteen
I changed my name
to Norma Jean O'Flaherty
and took off
for England Scotland Italy France
acting and reading
singing and living
drinking and loving,

Norma Jean O'Flaherty,

the girl with the famous name
and the dancing soul.

That's ten years ago.
I'm back in Dublin again, Dublin
incestuous dirty yattery wet.

I am who I was.
Not Norma Jean anymore.
Bernadette.'

Fan

'Sign dese buuks, ya little bastard,
   ya'd never know
       when I'd make a killin'
        outa ya!'

Milky chocolate

She said, 'Can you remember
if I ever slept with you?'
Joking? Wine
swam in her eyes.
'No, I can't remember,' I replied.
Her eyes wined, merciless and wise.
'Are you sure?' she persisted 'Am I not
familiar in certain ways?'
'I can't remember,' I repeated.
'Few things in life,' she said
'are quite as charming
as a highly developed
sense of forgetfulness.

It's the perfect way to kill remorse
which is a quite unnecessary curse.
I commend you for your sane
relationship with oblivion.
As for me, I'd rather eat chocolate
of the milky kind:
I like to be reminded
of the night you spoke
of things that seemed
the very sweetness of the mind.'

Lamping

Lamping in the Galtees
Ace saw foxes' eyes,
jewels piercing darkness,
vanish over ditches
like his efforts to love others.

Beethoven hopes

   I looked at the harvest moon.
It squatted in the accommodating sky
   like a pig in intervention.
   It was, at the same time,
going through its own kind of deconstruction
      beyond words
      beyond analysis
beyond the farthest reaches of any hitherto art.
Was it dreaming of a mind like a knife
   slicing out of the massive dark
   a fresh imitation of life?
Or was it just a bald old thing up there
      dreaming of hair?

Cold and golden and glowing,
   mocking my clouds of unknowing
it pigged in the homaging heavens
         and then, I swear,
         as I stood gaping there
it presented the Derridean cosmos
         with a breakthrough fart.

As the fart startled the universe
         I shivered at the thought
         of Beethoven hopes
               for prose and verse.
         O my dark Rosaleen
         dear Helen of Troy
         Eileen Aroon
new language is born to sing your praises
         thanks to the farting moon
               that loves the thinkers
         who won't use a word
         without making it absurd
               as a bird
                  whose song
                     chokes
on a perfectly argued academic turd.

My adjoining sexist

cocktails love with loathing, horror with delight,
cursing with praying:
'If it doesn't offend some stigmatical bitch
it's not worth saying.'

For adults

'Why are you so intent,' I asked, 'on getting
    other men's wives into bed?'

'Adultery is for adults,' he said.

Masterpieces

Mahler's No. 8 was on at the Point.
    Ace was smoking a joint
prior to having it off
with his favourite Administrator
who'd given up work, having landed the job.
    She just wanted to fuck
            and go crack
        with Mahler and Mozart
            far in the back-
                    ground.
    She tossed her raven head.
'That's what I love about masterpieces,' she said
'They're genuinely supportive of the real thing.'
    She smiled up at the ceiling
        neatly scratching her bum,
            comely as they come,
something of a masterpiece herself, stealing
into Ace's heart, lightly taking it over,
        creating there
    a more-than-musical feeling.

Home

'My father said if I played music in the streets
he'd kick me outa the house,
my rockanroll dream in my fist.
I left, leaving behind his angry eyes,
his curses and his cries.
I play the streets, the sometimes listening streets.
Home is where I harmonise.'

A possible solution

Best to take the bored fragments of self
      mould them into a story
that'll give a woman a bit of a laugh
      while she sees through me

The rain of May

In the heart of silence
speech limps behind music
mimicking the fall.

Music, silence, speech
help Ace
to have a ball.

And the rain of May pours blessing over all.

Seekers

Ace de Horner and Kanooce
love to stroll by the Dodder,
the pair o' them looking peaceful
yet capable of murder.

Ace is dressed in ancient Donegal tweed
and an ill-fitting IRA trenchcoat
which causes him to remember how people bleed
when tortured, knee-capped or simply blown up.

Kanooce looks at children and growls
as if he'd like to sample a couple for dinner.
Ace holds him tightly by the lead.

Thus do poet and dog amble, shuffle, prowl
together, the one seeking inspiration,
the other sniffing creation in search of food.

Poetry's future is in their paws. The signs are good
darkened though they be with stuff-o'-the-conscience blood.

Brothers

Ace de Horner likes to take Kanooce
out beyond Darndale into a field
at the back of a housing estate
weeping with unemployment
           and set him fighting
another pitbullterrier of equal ferocity
and stamina. In the breathless light
of bloodletting, far from the bad city,
the two dogs face each other
so savagely alike they might be brothers.
They are. Ace smokes his pipe and looks on.

(He has a modest tax-free bet on Kanooce to win.)

In slightly less than quarter of an hour
Kanooce has mincemeated his brother.
de Horner pats him on the head and toddles home.

(He's working on a poem about Original Sin.)

Real balls

At a party in Merrion Square
   or somewhere near there
Ace de Horner met a critic with real balls
   who'd shat upon his verses

in public. This was the sort of
   excremental response
that made Ace forget his dreams of skill
   and feel a dunce.

What the critic did not know was that
   Ace kept Kanooce in the Gents.
The critic drank, pronounced, revealed. Convinced
   he'd left de Horner feeling small

our critic chortled out to relieve himself.
   He met Kanooce in the loo.
Kanooce ate him, balls an' all.

Clearing

One evening, strolling through my heart,
picking my way through shapes of crack and hurt,
a twisty experience and I nearing
ninety, ignorant as ever of the art
of living, I lost my fragile bearings,
floundered about into a clearing,

stumbled on a gathering of distinguished
false gods. One, a grossly confident lump of meat,
was kissing his neighbour's hand
with slimey skill, drivelling 'This is fun! This is fun!'
The second was polishing his Ballymun
Moneylending Scheme For Needy Families
who might advance to Holidays In The Sun.
Another proclaimed the supremacy of bomb and gun.
The fourth expounded on the meaning of success
and failure. The fifth was eating and eating.
The sixth discoursed on True Style.
The next, an academic, was practising his smile
until his smile began to practise him
in a manner immemorially grim.
There were many others, all expert
confident gods squatting on their behinds.
I, being cowardly, greeted them.

       They acknowledged my greeting
and welcomed me to the lewd
babble of their monthly meeting,
a self-adoring atmosphere with a strong appeal
shaped into a question: Is this real? Unreal?
I sat in the middle of the clearing and looked around.
Was I lost or found?

O suave explainers

Where the terrors come from no one knows
though I've tasted the explainers at their
work of telling me the origin of the noose
and the black arts matting what's left of my hair.

But no explainer will clarify the boy
waiting for me at the corner of a street
who ran at me, ran at me
and tried to knife me. He did not

nor will he try it again.
Minutes later, a woman, hostile at first,
asked me home for tea.

I went. There was no tea. There was a man
so frozen with terror he reminded
me of me.

That evening, at moments which I can't explain,
I spoke of what I'd seen and done.
They listened, asked me to go.

I went. Who are they? Who was the boy?
Where is the knife? Why will he never use it again?
O suave explainers, tell me what I should know
for you thrive up there like terror, and I am here below.

The stuff

Ace de Horner developed a Miltonic ambition
to write an epic for the Irish race,
involving many distinguished gods and goddesses
passionate and talented though frequently disgraced,
abandoning their divine nature
to become shitty politicos and shrewd clerics
profiting from the soul's ordure.

Well, that's the stuff of epics.

Once before

In his Bluebell cell, Ace, broody alone,
    Picked his nose.
    From his fingertips there rose
A flowersplinter of Shakespeare's backbone
Which he'd seen once before in the Women's Marathon.

Garlic

MacAnnassbie's jokes are memorable as garlic.
Is there anyone alive he hasn't mocked?
'What do a fridge and a woman have in common?'
'I don't know, MacAnnassbie.'
'They both leak when they're fucked.'

Blue barrier

The night Ace broke the blue barrier
he learned a lot about money,
slept with a slightly bleeding woman
who loved to talk dirty.

There was a mad drive through rain
flailing down on Ireland
like a drinker pissing in dust
raising a few bubbles

bulgingpopping like a politician's
lies
on paper radio satellite telly
and other organs of disease.

Into this room came Ace de Horner
where every word was polished clean,
he wolfed the Kildare lamb
and sang obscene

songs till the slightly bleeding
woman showed him her token.
The rain pounded the starless dark.
Ace sang to his magical mark.
The blue barrier was broken.

The sound

Only the silence will not be borne.
Come on, what's the gossip, scandal, start joking,
make the sound that justifies our being born,
the Adam sound that wards off choking.

Gentleman

A gentleman to the core, whatever the core is;
flawless manners, perfect accent, first-class brain
content, at evening, to drink with Dolores
nectar from the skulls of the slain.

Open window

A girl's delighted scream thrilled in
    through the open window,
        late Summer night,
        Ace sitting on his own
    pondering two pairs of scissors
pens tapes books paper diary globe
    bible radio phonebook phone.
It doesn't matter, his blood sang for
        one startling instant,
it doesn't matter, it doesn't matter.
He was never happier than in that moment,
        nor more alone.

How may one know precisely?

Like a bad winter hobbling off
    into another time, another place,
like a fly jerkily moving across
    an old dog's sleeping face,
like Ambrose Callan begging, limping
    from callous place to place
Ace drags hacked body and soul
    towards a state of grace.

Jesus, he's fit to laugh at himself,
    he's such a clown,
such a parody of what he might dream he is,
    such a victim of such a notion,

when he says 'grace', the word swims
                in his head,
    will he laugh or cry?
The fly quits the dog's face, Ambrose Callan sleeps,
in a corner of time the bad winter lies down to die.

How may one know precisely why not to ask why?

Outings

When Ace goes into that land beyond language
he knows silences are cries.
When he returns, words are stranger than ever
and he laughs aloud at his own lies.

One of these will rock forever

Then Ace rose up
    and took the boat and the bike
        to Sellafield
          to rock
against the nuclear devils in their bunkers
   and the clean progressive thinkers.
It was the longest day of that year
      or any year
      and Ace rocked
like an eagle gone mad in the sky
like a scientist discovering words
like a Christian homosexual proving
they were all at it in the Old Testament
like seven naked children splashing in a pond
in a garden somewhere in Dublin
like three knives that have never stabbed
      anyone yet
like the ticktock of a clock that soon will refuse
      to ticktock anymore
like a sixteen-year-old lad on the threshold of whiskey
      sure/unsure at the pub door
like an old teacher who knows in a moment
   he has never taught anyone anything
and has learned that learning is what remains
when all the books have been forgotten
like Mary Ellen dying in bed on a Sunday afternoon
swearing to Christ she'll not salute the bastards
even if she meets them in heaven
like a helicopter falling in love with the sea
introducing the millionaire pilot to the mermaid
in a sunwonder of wind and wave
like a feast of winter fleas hotting it up in a beggar's coat
like an old actor in his cage of egotism
abusing Shakespeare for writing what he never wrote
like five thousand foetuses aborted from five
thousand Irish women
doing their own little bloody abandoned dance
in the middle of the poisoned Irish Sea
'O mammy show me the way to go home
I'm tired and I wanna go to bed
I had a little drink about an hour ago
and it's gone right to my head'
like a hundred boys in the Orphans' Band

dressed in green swastikas in Croke Park
playing music that has countless thousands weeping
like all the plastic bags we can't get rid of
like the cutie-sweetie victim talk
of leukaemia children in Dundalk
like the Christmas bargain-hunters keeping
their balls and fannies warm in midnight frost
because cut-price colour television is all the go
although the names of all our wicked uncles have been lost
like all the ceasefires ceasefires ceasefires
like all the stories opening Once, a long time ago
       that's how
         Ace rocked
         at the gates
             of nuclear
               Sellafield
until the blood ran down his love and protest
         and blinded his eyes
         but
         he rocked
         blind an' all as he was
         rocked and rocked
         till no one and nothing remained
         but himself and
         the evil thing
         the pleasant plausible evil thing.
One of these will rock forever.
  One of these will always sing.
Don't ask Ace, there's blood on his face
  and he's still rocking.

Written on paper stuck to a tattered coat

'Although his genius is devoted to a bomb
He won't stop the blessing kissing the palm.'

Smelly craters

Ace climbed and climbed
until he reached the moon.
He searched black fields for Buckteeth Liz
but she was gone
although her smell filled every crater
like fish in the noonday sun.

When lights turn red

'Clean your windscreen, misther?' queries the boy
in the green cap,
the wiper ready in his fist.
'No! No!' snaps the motorist.

A dead rat lands in his lap.

University

'My name is Scud Gallivan. I was
sexually assaulted at the back of a pub in
Mallow in October seventy-four
by a tinker, a big stinkin' bully of a man
    who tore into me like a storm.
I killed him. I'll never know how, but I killed
him though he was nearly twice my size.
I got eight years in Mountjoy prison.

"Welcome to our University of crime,"
          smiles a rapist
    on my very first day.
          For three years
          I wrote a play
    (they called it tragi-comedy).

          Writing the play
taught me I was homosexual too.

    I did five years.

One wenchy summer night in Ballybofey
I assaulted a young tinker, killed him.
They'll get me. Meanwhile, I know what to do.'

Intruder

Pardon me, Ace, if I intrude now and then.
I'm one of the people you meet in the streets,
one of the shuffling men
with, I think, something to say.

I'll face you, say it, shuffle away.

Would Ireland know?

' "And what's so wrong with a United Ireland?"
asked the fat poet. He quoted a few lines,
my soul expanded like a rubber band,
I sensed alternatives, I read the signs

while half-ashamed of my murderous youth
when snake-sectarian hatred was my god
commanding me to kill the other kind.
I did, got life, my world's this prison-yard

where, frosty mornings, I scratch my balls
thinking of smoked salmon, brown bread, chilled wine,
cigars, French brandy, women, United Ireland.

The fat poet pays monthly social calls,
reads me sad love-poems, we get on fine
together. One day, he feels, I'll understand.

Meanwhile I wonder, coping with prison rot,
would Ireland know if 'twere united or not?
Poemreader, friend of freedom, don't answer that.'

Killing the singers

I

As a result of an heroic performance
by a few dedicated sportsmen
with a tartar killing lust in the blood
two plastic bags full of dead songbirds
were found in a Wicklow wood.

Thrushes linnets blackbirds robins larks
          some of heaven's sweetest singers
were shot by sportsmen practising their skill
          in the Garden of Ireland.

The smaller the bird, the sportsmen say, the sweeter the kill.

I would like these birds to be born again,
to be singing, to strike me as free,
spontaneous, innocent, flitting, soaring the skies,
and then, for food, when they're tired and hungry from singing
   I'd like to see prepared for them
        and elegantly presented
                an inventive feast
made of these dedicated sportsmen's eyes.

Like songbirds, this moment, I sing you no lies.

II

The birds of Mexico protest
at the slaughter of their Irish cousins;
Hear the Red-tailed Hawk, Scaled Quail, Mourning Dove,
Barn Owl, Poor Will, Ladder-backed Woodpecker,
Horned Lark, Curve-billed Thrasher, Rough-winged Swallow,
Scott's Oriole, Blue Bunting, Yellow Warbler,
Summer Tanager, Long-tailed Hermit, Black-throated Sparrow,
Brush Finch, Rock Wren, Black-tailed Gnatcatcher,
Common Cardinal, Yellowhead Blackbird, Groove-billed Ani,
Blue Honeycreeper, Longspar, Yucatan Jay,
Common Pottoo, White-necked Raven, Lovely Cotinga,
Black Skimmer, Loggerbead Shrike, Painted Redstart,
Golden Vireo, Bell's Warbler, Aztec Parakeet

all, in their angry protest, all complete.

III

Last night in Leeson Street I met
a killer of songbirds. He was
tanned and handsome.
I asked him
why he found it necessary
to kill the singers.
He said with a grin
that killing helped him
keep his eye in.

Sniper

Usually, Sniper sits up in the hills
but yesterday was so hot
he felt a bit dizzy by late
afternoon, a buzz of ills
sickfizzled his head. Today
he squats in a bombed-out hotel
on the lip of hell.
Cooler here.

                    What'll I try now?
Children? Women? Anything that moves?
There's somebody sitting in the shade
of a ruin, dark triangles, gashed. Yes, friend.

                    Simple enough.
This is like peeping through a keyhole,
I can kill anyone in the room
from people making trouble to people making love.

A fierce healing

Ace is determined that he's not going
to take the rap
for the fact that he was born with a severe
dose of pre-natal clap.

His life is a fierce healing of a disease
he never understood
although he sometimes feels it creeping,
crawling, slithering through his blood.

Why then should anyone be surprised to see
him lurching against walls
as if he were stealing the whitewash off them?
If he sees life as a festival

at times, a plague at others, well, that is
easy to understand
but sometimes he vanishes into mountains
or cities in some distant land

and one simply has to wait for him
to return.
He does, not mentioning where he's been,
looking lost and forlorn

for a while but picking up in time
to continue his strange war
against what happened before he was born,
the dictates of his own star

hovering-quivering with ancient and future
meanings and questions above his head.
What is sickness? Health? The gift of healing?
Ace in silence closes his eyes and listens

to voices, voices: Heal me, O Lord, and I
shall be healed. Love him with all your heart and mind.
Drowned boys of summer rot in the scotfree sea.
Heal me, O Lord, as darkness wraps the land.

Given the city and the season

On one of those icy Christmassy nights in Dublin
when the chill invades even the cosiest feet
an old culchie whose life had known some trouble
died of the cold in a laneway off O'Connell Street

and lay there, his hands around his head
in a gripped huddle for three days
before Ace de Horner and Kanooce found him
as they muled out on their wandering ways.

Kanooce sniffed the old man
and grabbed a bite out of his frozen face.
de Horner chastised him, 'Tch! Tch! Naughty dog!
Naughty dog!
How dare you behave like that!
How dare you bite the cold corpse
of an old wretch up in Dublin from the bog?'

Kanooce pithung his head and continued to chew.
Given the city and the season that were in it,
    what else could the poor dog do?

Ultimate Peace

Looking into Kanooce's eyes
Ace de Horner swore he loved
the pitbullterrier's music,
savage, gripping, spontaneous.

'O dear Kanooce,' sighed Ace
'Where would I be without your music?
How could I face this callous world
devoid of sensitivity and grace?

All my poor music is a tribute to yours.
All my poems exist to sing
of the music you bring to everything
in light, in dark, both in and out of doors.

What is your magic, dear Kanooce, what is your magic?
No one can explain it.
No human can attain it
and yet your magic has its own peculiar logic.'

Kanooce, pitgrinning, looked at Ace.
Take me for a walk, he said, or seemed to say.
So off they flopped along our local Appian Way
like a pair of convent girls in a state of grace.

Such music, then, vibrated from that pair
people stood and listened;
their hearts thrilled, their eyes glistened
and the ultimate peace of poetry was everywhere.

Estuary woman

Three gone. She wept. Life is a child.
Her belly kicked, kicked.
She smiled.
Outside, a feather
drifted with the tide.

Secret

At an early age, gravy-stained, bread-seeking, Ace learned
the secret of the dance:
flow with the music, the half-chance.

Sins of the fathers

Ace watched the sins of the fathers take over the beach:
one stuck his hands in his floppy trousers pockets
one stared at a chocolate-finger stuck in ice-cream
one held a green towel poised above the sand
one played with a son, he knew it was his son
one reclined in a fabricated blue tent
one swung a stick at a small yellow ball
one ran looking for something to hide from
one tested his toes on recalcitrant gravel
one played with a make-believe pink lifebelt
one tooted his horn, 'twas a cheeky toot
one walked forever at the edge of the tide
one covered himself up as if it were winter
one climbed stone steps, her tongue hanging out.

To no one

Her husband passed on the street outside.
She watched, said softly to no one:
'The things you'd see passin' the window
When you wouldn't have a gun.'

The challenge of vanishing faces

Ace made a barrel for himself.
Harvey finished the gun.
That night on the banks of the Grand Canal
They tripped over the moon
And x-rayed the lazy, cratered faces
That vanished in the light of dawn.

Enterexit

In she came, sat, cried. God knows
how long she wept before she left the room.
Her tears remained and spoke. Outside, the waves
were crazy children foaming at the moon.

Query

'At play in the fields of the Lord,
Dark Rose, to the end of the world.'

My friend wants to know who wrote that.

'I found it in a drawer in his desk.'

I don't know.
It doesn't matter.
He made it his own
before he went down

        to play in the fields that wait
                for the end of the world.

Dark Rose. Young man.

Tired

So tired now, I can hear the language
within the language they're hawking
all around me.

So tired, I must sit and listen
deep-inside to what they say:
love is murder, love is laughter,
      Francis Madden
      loves his cousin
      that way.

Now and then

'May we fuck?' he said to many women he met.
Got Arctic looks, slaps on the face, clatters on the head.
Now and then, to his surprise, a not
unbeautiful woman joined him in bed.
'Why?' he whispered. 'Insolent pig' she said.

Pondering the situation

Honesty in ink is one thing but honesty
in blood is quite another, thought lousyluck
Ace as the lady confronted him
and proceeded to call him the crook
of crooks, shyster of shysters, conman to outdo
all conmen. He heard himself agreeing with her.
She grew more eloquent, vile and true,
he more timid, swallowing her abuse like beer,
the golden foreign stuff you see in the ads
and want to wallow in, fill your bath with

before venturing forth on a truth-telling expedition of your own,
walking up to a strange woman accompanied by a lad
who can't cope with your belligerent, drunken myth
as you steal the woman from in front of his face
                and hiccup her home
                to your honest bed.
All this ran through Ace de Horner's head
as the lady wiped the street with him
then dumped him in a plastic bag, tied it
                and threw it in a bin.
    Ace is hiding there at the moment
                pondering the situation,
                taking it all in.

Hellwellwisher

'I know you rise
bright an' early
to write your poetry.

Why? You'd be
better off
attending to me

here in this
pearl bedroom
smelling of piss

and old prayers
but I also know
the road you must go

to find what you
hope to find:
something small, hard, true,

impossible
to get into words.
So good luck and go to hell.'

Bikeman

I

Who is that bikeman
savaging my sleep?
Roar, roar, he roars
up and down the road
outside my door,
stopping there
to flash his lights
his threatening lights
through my bedroom,
through my mind
like a white, busy
violating knife.

Should I get up
and accost him?
Or should I let him
roar and roar until he goes
away?

I fall asleep
and become, for the first
time in my life
(as far as I know)
a strong, sure, deliberate
murderer.

I have this blue, small rock
in my hands
and I am battering the head
of a complete stranger.
Someone tries to stop me.
I rock his brains out
on the handy gravel.
Then I go on battering
the black helmeted head
until there's nothing left
but a squelch of bones
and blood and dirt
in the handy gravel.

It is the bloody dirt
I love, the bikeman's
blood and dirt, the
bikeman's battered head.

And I have never known
such pleasure!
How come murder is so pleasant?
So fragrant? So satisfying?
Of course, this is all
in my sleep, and when I wake
daylight will greet me
with its understandable breakfast –
bread of guilt
milk of remorse
tears I shall be fit to drink.
For the moment, however,
in this dear barbaric sleep
I have rid the world
of one arrogant, persistent,
systematic, brazen
violator of peace.
Therefore, I thank the small blue rock.
Therefore, I am happy.
Therefore, I do not weep.

II

Next morning,
listening to the happy squeals
of children in the sea
which may roar its might
tonight or tomorrow night,
seeing the slow shuffle
of an old man through
sand and gravel,
the intricate dance
of the sun's magnanimous rays,
I know the sanest way to live
is to try to perfect
a clear, intense,
discriminating style of praise.

Well, as the man said, that'd be grand.

The change

'We were screwing away happily this morning
when her friend Agnes rang and said
I was screwing three other women as well.
Jesus! The change Agnes made in the bed!'

A small, white card

'You have five minutes to evacuate this building!'
    The voice was urgentloud
    Yet careful not to shout.
Ace wandered the corridors, went
    downstairs upstairs sideways
    seeking the sign WAY OUT.
He met a girl from Bosnia
holding a small white card that said
    'I'm a refugee, please
    give me money for food.'
She had long pale fingers, as if without blood.
Ace searched his pockets, a pound, gave it to her.
    She smiled.
    He smiled.
They sat together, saying nothing
    there
in what was suddenly the quietest
    corner of town.
Love's appetite was fed in evacuated London.

A pair o' them in it

' "This day thou art with me in Paradise."
So the thief with the good word was saved from hell,
went to heaven. But what of ould snarlygob?
I hope the ould bollocks went up as well.'

Resting place

For years Lorna has felt outcast.
Doesn't know why she's so depressed.
Ace, sleeping between her breasts,
travels north south east and west.
What is love for two when one is lost?
Lorna heats beneath. Ace is blessed
For now. Who in the end has, is, truly kissed?
And who will know the taste of waste?

The woozy sun

Ace de Horner is compiling an anthology
    in which he'll include
his friends, all masters of the exquisite
    lyric, nothing crude,

to be translated into the very eastest
    of East European tongues.
The sun rises there. It'll sink to rest,
    woozy with our songs.

The stars are hammers

The old priest reads his poems
    in and out of prison
    for forty years.
He believes in peace.

Up comes the singer,
    a lark in winter
    thrills out his heart
denouncing war.

And here's a young woman
    beaten up so many times
    she knows how to survive.
Surviving, she knows

why the priest and the singer
    are one voice.
There's an audience of millions.
    Rejoice!

In the icy streets I meet
    a woman, crying.
We go for a drink.
    'He just keeps on drinking

but he never beats me up.
    He's full of himself, full
of himself. I want him to love me, fuck me.
    He drinks. I want him. That's all.'

On the bridge, as always, a child begs.
    No. He lies there, all eyes in the night,
    a small boy,
cold, strangely exquisite

as if a cruel genius had sculpted him
    and placed him there in the cold
to tell us whatever we're bold enough to hear.
    What do I hear?

What do I see? The stars are hammers
    in the hands of an enraged thing.
Hunger endures. So do full bellies
    and hearts that sing.

Back there

In the streets, ice grips the roots of my hair.
I turn and look directly down the street.
Did someone kill me back there?

Friend

' 'Tis only an old skull,' said Ace, 'that once
                    contained ideas, music, song.
Nothing to fear from it, I'd rather have it for a friend
                    than many a living tongue.'
I looked at the skull: old gasgob, eyehole, greybone.
                    My own.

That picture

At an early age, Ace de Horner set out to find
himself. It was a rambling scrambling kind of search
and it led Ace into many a hole in the ground,
dicey encounters with Church and State
and many a boisterous night and morning in Dublin pubs,
arguing with latchikoes, knockers and yobs.
One morning, at a revolting twist
in his head, Ace penetrated a winter mist
and found himself in the muck of the Fairview slobs.
He stood back and looked at himself.
                    A grisly sight
yet not without a certain mucky charm.
In fact, there and then, he photographed himself.
Frequently now, in Bluebell, in what passes for a flat,
he studies that picture with a fond smile
and an increasing sense of alarm.

Everest

Ace de Horner stayed in bed with Molly for three days.
Molly had a thin body, apparently fragile
yet blessed with stamina that amazed Ace
whose IRA trenchcoat sat on a windowsill
like a tricktoy witness of their love-making.
This was spiritual food to the poet
whose life seemed a sustained sexual diet
longing for vitamins
until Molly taught him the delights of loving
or revived a love that was in love with dying
('O fuck me, Ace, till I'm screaming and crying').
Late in the third night, without quitting bed
(apart from briefish periods we all understand)
they climbed an Everest of loving where
nobody, it seemed, had ever soared before
(such is the arrogance of enmeshed flesh).
                                        After,
Molly kissed Ace's prick (it looked like gratitude
but in fact 'twas farewell), scratched his head
(a groggy concoction after three daysnights in bed),
told his fortune from the palm of his hand
(mullarkey about a tricky wizard going blind),
then the pair o' them collapsed in a fit of laughter.

Molly went to live in a distant land.
Ace brooded on what it means to be healthy
when he wasn't chewing the fruits of being lonely.
Molly made a fortune telling the fortunes
of love-smitten groping creatures
lusting for a destiny. Molly knew her past,
had few doubts about her future

in which there could be no place
for Ace, poor Ace,
poor, broody, sensitive, poem-smitten Ace.

And what man in his right mind
would blame a woman
who'd toyed
            with the vision
                    of a tricky
                        wizard
                            going
                                blind?

Looking

Provisional in bed, eyes cool and blue,
'Don't come looking for me,' she said.
'If there's looking to be done
It'll be me for you.'

A new metre

Ace de Horner loves to run amok among
metres in a way that may produce
the sort of song
he's hungered for since fanatical youth
when he heard words and hoofbeats dancing
on a Five Lamps fair-day morning
cattle slipping, men encouraging,
urging him to pursue elusive magic
through the hot, damp shames of growing up.
Since every madness has its logic
Ace seeks in metre to beat the rap
of casual despair in days and nights
and mornings crawling with a gallows will.
There's no metre, modern or ancient, he doesn't know
(where do they come from? where must they go?)
or cannot use with sticky skill.
Gay hexameters flash their lights,
trochees, spondees fall like snow
    on a nameless hill
            until
Kanooce chomps in, starving, some black day
    and starts to eat
the toes off Ace's succulent metrical feet.
    Down Kanooce's gullet they go –
hexameters, spondees, trochees, alexandrines
    like Longford dogfood
    and best wines.

Ace watches in despair and must endure it.
It doesn't happen often, thanks be to God
    and the shocked Muses
but when it does happen, Ace, appalled, bears witness
    to the jaws of this metre-chewing monster.
He knows extreme internal pain
watching his poem vanish down Kanooce's drain.
    He agonises as he sees
    sonnets epigrams villanelles
            chunks of epics
            lyrics pure as bells

        disappear

    into that devouring maw
            that knows no law
            but its own
    which I'd rather not try to define.
        And yet
as Ace stands, and looks, and listens,
        slowly, inevitably,

    a new metre is born
in the chewing music of Kanooce's jaws,
    a metre stranger
than the harmony of the spheres
which it renders rather tame.

        This new
        ecstatic
    callous barbaric
        metre

is Ace's music for a moment

    and if he can
through skill and right devotion
    word-incarnate
that creative crime

    it may be yours
        and mine

        in time.

A workable clarity

Ace de Horner's vision of Ireland is nicely
   split and splitting.
He always speaks derisively of
   North and South. Instead, he mentions

Sorth and Nouth, territories occupied
   in his wordscape by
   Protholics and Catestants
   as they live and die

in the shat-on beauty of their island.
Noyalists and Lashionalists picnic together
in all kinds of weather,
chewing tarpition sandwiches with sugto.
Ace confesses confusion, believing that he
will, round some bend, achieve a workable clarity.

Being clear, he sees, is a dangerous business.
One could be murdered for lucidity
in that island where yes is no and no is yes
so often. Yet he persists, works, scribbles from inside
himself, Kanooce chomping like Cuchulain at his side,
never afraid to face the incoming or outgoing tide.

Poetry Conference

The onlookers grin; he plans Pythagoras;
   the abandoned poem sinks on one knee;
Ace de Horner sinks into a glass
   and drinks the sea.

What they saw

Ace accosted the blind poets of Ireland
at a Poets' Disco in Dumb Cat:
blind Willy blind Paddy blind Mikey
blind Thady blind Biddy blind Matt

blind Raftery blind Scattery blind Carolan
blind Baldy blind Scourge blind Cripes
blind Limerick blind Kerry blind Monaghan
blind Balor blind Angel blind Tripe

and countless blind others prodded their way
through themselves, each other, the disco.

'Sing up,' shouted Raftery, 'We've nothing to say,
nothing to offer but bloody blind gusto.'

So they sang till the halls of Dumb Cat rang
like a dream of inspired voices
and the island of Ireland began to see
the visionary head is the heart that rejoices
in the blind night, in the blind light
of morning, noon, afternoon.

'Sing up,' sang Raftery, 'We put nothing right
but we'll show you the sun dancing with the moon.'

And that's what they saw when they sang
of the darkness, the light, the road to Dumb Cat.
Ace de Horner closed his eyes, blind man
for a while, beginning to know where he's at,

beginning to see how the blind poets see him
with eyes like pale skies, calling the tune
that Ace knows he can dance to forever,
and no one for company but the sun and the moon.

Madrigal Sweeney

He came out of the trees
a swinging, bald, tarzanian god
ebullient with mysteries
the copious mid-air his true abode,

Madrigal Sweeney, our most translated lunatic,
mouth frothing with primal juice,
shouting as he hurled from branch to branch
'Kanooce! Kanooce! I want Kanooce!'

until he came at last to the Bluebell pad,
stood trembling at the door, bleeding and mad
and eager to be pleased.

Kanooce came out and bit his shaking face
his hands his legs his tears his grin his sweat.
Too much bitten, Sweeney sought the trees.

From his asylum, bleedingwounded there,
'Kanooce! Kanooce! I want Kanooce!' pleads down the air,

cry of a lost creature for a somehow brother.
Bite, cry try to translate each other.

A matter of glimpses and tiny sounds

Ace went to a brothel with Kanooce.
As they entered the brothel, three policemen,
cosy in a new Toyota Carina
photographed poet and beast.
Nearly all the women were pleasant and plump
and far too versatile for Ace.
One woman, Connemara Bridie, touched him
and said it was no disgrace
for a poet to be having it off
with a girl of her humble origins
and he mustn't worry, he wasn't committing

any kind of sin,
he was just going to have
the whopper of a time,
far from the bad, boring world of business, money,
poetry, scribbling, guff, bluster, critics and crime.
Ace smiled shakily as Connemara Bridie
took his clothes off.
In no time at all, she
was making love
to the sad master of iambic pentameter
through whose head
loveliness gushed like the Liffey in spate
but slowly melted in Bridie's skilled and busy arms
working the cold wastes of the poet's body
with qualified sagacity and charm.
In a brief, ecstatic time
Ace entered Bridie
who was varied and real
as the oldest part of the Bible
read by living and dead eyes
but understood (you'd swear) only
by those who know they know nothing
about God
and are hungry
for hints hopes anecdotes clues rumours yarns
told by strangers in dubious pubs
to some who tend to live beyond bounds.
I suppose it's a matter of glimpses and tiny sounds.
Connemara Bridie smiled at the poet.
He had done his best
and found what felt like love
at a stranger's breast,
a kind of poetry.
Ace handed Bridie some money.
Kanooce growled a titan growl.
Ace thought he was going to bite
Bridie but Kanooce bounded
up the stairs of the brothel
into a room where a man sat
smugly, Sir Paddy Pimp, waiting.
Kanooce bit him once, then bit him a lot,
in fact chewed a lump of thigh
before flumping down the stairs.
It has never been suggested by anyone
that Kanooce has ever practised airs
or graces, but as he passed by

Connemara Bridie, he raised his head
in pitbull homage, and made as if to salute
the pleasant woman who giggled
'Jeepers! Isn't he cute!'

          Then out into the night
went Ace and Kanooce
past the three policemen
in their virginal Toyota,
still taking photographs
of the poet and his beastly warrior.
Would these photographs
be shown to all the nation
on the front page
of the *Funday Sindependent?*
Or would they be reserved
for birthday parties
of Superintendents and Sergeants
at the Station?

I've never figured that one out.
Kanooce and Ace went home to the Bluebell pad,
the poet reflecting
how that evening,
more than most,
had been a mixture of good and bad

and left him feeling very far from sad.

How and why till you're blue with the flu

How does a lover feel when a lover calls?
Like a woman, like a man.
Why does a dog lick his own balls?
Because he can.

Bird's Custard

Ace is visited by exultant moments
when he rejoices in his unquestionable uselessness,
the uselessness of poetry to which his seventh sense
tells him he's committed, more or less.

The joy of uselessness kills his guilt
for a while. It's like pissing in a cup
and tossing the piss out the window
like a blessing on humanity.

Or it's like standing at traffic-lights
in one of the busiest streets in Dublin.
Ace relishes complete futility,

appalling slavishness of everyone going
nowhere in some style. A man is getting out
of his car, he's approaching a woman in the car

ahead of him, he's red in the face, this man, he's cursing
her like well-dressed hell, she's starting to cry,
he huffs back to his wheel, the man has won his war.

If Kanooce were here, thinks Ace, he'd eat the bastard
but the lazy tyke is at home, milling his Bird's Custard.

On Dalkey Hill

The speculators had made a killing
on the devalued pound
and were having a party
to celebrate their good fortune.

They held a Masked Ball
on Dalkey Hill.
They wore masks of wolves skunks tigers rats
foxes ferrets. It was beautiful.

It was thrilling, a sophisticated
yet primitive way to celebrate
their style of making a killing. (It's all
about style, darling.) The party went on late

into the night, later still
into the following day.
Ace de Horner and Kanooce went out walking.
They passed that way.

When Kanooce saw the rats and ferrets
the foxes tigers skunks wolves
he cut loose, he started eating
them, feasting on buttocks, on calves
of legs, on bits of belly too.
The speculators had not bargained for this.
Some of them pissed in dread.
Kanooce lapped their piss

for he was thirsty from gobbling their meat
and Dalkey piss is like wine.
What a scene that was, what a scene!
Back in the Bluebell pad, Kanooce stretched out by the fire,

gorged with pissy lumps of speculators.
de Horner brooded on the meaning of it all,
thought of writing a poem about being too fond of money
and how this might account for our fall

from grace. And why, he wondered, wear animal-masks
when you go for a dance and a feast?
Kanooce was snoring happily. How much of the meat
of moneymen was changing to shit in the belly of the beast?

Staring at Kanooce, Ace brooded on these things
and concluded there was no answer.
Then he, too, fell asleep by the fire and dreamed
of a masked, confident, succulent dancer

dancing on Dalkey Hill
bacchanalian Dalkey Hill
where the sun is allowed to shine
and the rain privileged to fall.

Furniture

'He's one of the richest men in the country
but my Jesus he's liable to lose the head
if the drink buckles him. He
might stagger in here to this room, the bad
look in his eye, stand in the middle o' the floor,
size up the price of every piece o' furniture
and then, because there's some piece he doesn't admire,
break everything in the room,
                              scattering
the smashed pieces everywhere.
                              Next day
he comes back, not, as you might expect,
                              penitent,
but willin' to pay, yessir, willin' to pay
twice or three times the value of what he
destroyed. And people take it because he buys
their anger and hatred. He smiles and goes away.
There's plenty furniture to break some later day.'

Saint Augustine Street

Ace met a man in Saint Augustine Street.
The blackguard years had mugged his head.
Ace knew him and didn't know him.
'We were there together,' the man said.

Beards

Ace grew a beard, cut it, grew it, cut it again.
His attitude to beards wavered
like his faith in men.

The man he is

Ace being the man he is does what he does
in the way that is his alone.
He writes, writes, seeking the elusive buzz
that wasps and butterflies his marrowbone,
    gentle, ferocious waves and surges
uttering his dreams, piled prehistoric urges
as he casts his eye on his IRA trenchcoat
unscorched by petrol-bomb, unmarked by bullet,
happy to hang on the wall of the Bluebell pad,
happy to hang like a Kevin Barry lad.

    Yet Ace likes corridors
far from testing mountains and cathartic moors,
corridors' reticent, deadly whisperings.
His hearing-aid is a great help in this
and makes him look like a great poet too,
distinguished, a little deprived, eagle-sharp,
vigilant, eager to hear, attentive as hell,
nodding in meticulous understanding, slow to carp
and witty as well.

The corridors like him and conserve his whisperings
like jewels in darkness. They'll come to light in time,
shining and resonant as Ace's *Bluebell Songs*,
as yet unwritten sources of his fame.

Meanwhile, Ace is happy to murmur his own name,
being the man he is, the man
who plays several leading parts in his own plan,
his own poem, his own play.
He knows there is, being the man he is, no other way.

At least, that's the man he is today.

On loan from heaven

Ace is a prim little prick much of the time
loving to show how sensitive he is. He is.
To this end, he has perfected an attractive stammer
which he sweats out of hiding at moments of crisis.

Hard would he be of heart who'd fail to respond
to Ace's perfectly wounded soul
stammering into your understanding
                       and beyond
into spiritregions absolvingly beautiful

where you realise you're a clumsy man, woman
in the presence of a stammering angel
on loan from heaven for your olderliefest sake.

Belt up; let the angel explain
what's happening, be open to the full
truth and don't be embarrassed by your mistakes.

Here's a stammering man who has never lied.
Stammering heaven is on his side. Did I
call him a prim little prick? Sorry. That was
bitchy, figgy and unforgivably snide.

Am I forgiven? Only Ace de Horner can decide.

The Sin of the World

Out by Kilmainham, one evening in winter
    (why had certain houses fallen down?)
Ace de Horner strode with Kanooce,
               uglier than ever.
They came to a twist in the road,
    rounded it to see a thick, black cloud
bearing down on them, the blackest thing
they'd ever seen. Not even in his most

devil-riddled dreaming
(such as the modest
movement of curtains
that showed some reasons
for Asia's agony)
had Kanooce witnessed such a huge black face
and body that yet were no body and face.
    Ace halted, froze in recognition.
'It's the sin of the world,' his words fell and broke
on Kanooce's head. The sin of the world.
Not for nothing does Ace believe
Kanooce is the bravest dog in Christendom.
Kanooce leaped at the sin of the world
and began to chew the blackness
            but the more
            he ate it
the more it continued to grow,
outstripping the future, gulping the long ago.

At last, exhausted, his belly bulging with sin
            Kanooce gave up.
            How could he know
there was no end to it all, no end?
The black cloud scowled and growled and grew
till it covered Dublin first, then all Ireland.
        All that black strangling
            All that green!
            Obscene!

        What could the poet do?

He walked straight through it. That's what he did.

I have my strength, he thought, I have my pride
my words may live, my body will rot,
I'll walk right through it.
        He did
                and came out the other side,
            changed
in ways he couldn't begin to understand
no matter how hard he looked
at the cut and the go of his greenblack land.
        At his heels, Kanooce persisted
            like flu in winter.
That's a helluva lot of sin, thought Ace,
yet I'm not disgusted
at the thought, at the sight. I cannot speak

like a holy seer
but sin is here
and here is sin
call it any name you will
and I must try not to live in fear
though not a day goes by but we kill
each other, deepening that black face,
black body that is no body, no face.
Not even Kanooce in all his rage
could eat it. It grows and grows eternally
but so does the poor poetry of men
and women stalking the blackness,
wading through it, coming out again
where small words smile and caress
the stragglers, wanderers lost in themselves,
helping them along
till in the distance
someone hears
a sound
that will become a song:

> Live in the black cloud
> walk through the black cloud
> work in the black cloud
> love in the black cloud
>
> the words that told your truth
> are the same words when you lied
> come out the other side
> come out the other side

Ace heard the song
and started to hum it,
leading Kanooce
through the shadowed town
of Dublin loving fun.

(Why had certain houses fallen down?)

The moving people

The statue looked at the people and thought
'Why are they all moving about?'

Shakespeare and crisps

The silent majority are a noisy lot, thought
Ace, venturing down a street
into a theatre where the stage was set
for *A Midsummer-Night's Dream*
in mid-winter. Crisps and peanuts
were available in the theatre bar
and many customers, e'er the play began,
filled their bellies with beer
which meant they were pissing
throughout the first act. It was a nightmare
for Ace who was fit to scream.
                 He changed seats.
The couple in front were chatting
like Saddams. He saw but couldn't hear
the play. Bad. Bad dream.
   If only the silent majority stayed silent,
he thought, Shakespeare might be with us a moment
but whenever these words have a chance to fly about
crisps, beer and peanuts knock 'em out.

Our hero quit the theatre, into the town,
   compelled-content
in that fastfood noisy sea, to drown.

Is it any wonder people think he's a clown?

How much pig?

How much pig lives in your average man?
What sparking grunt ignites his lyric whine
when he confesses to a woman
she has driven him to write
love-poems to split a reader's heart

and then subside into a wounded silence?
What element of pig empowers his fist
when he asserts mangodly rules of violence?

And if the pig is there why will he not
see that snouty hunk of brute
within himself? Why lie about the fact?

Is it because he's the ablest of the lot?
A spiritcritic with a lust for truth
clouded at times by necessary tact?

Or does he tell himself he must expel
his brother to a scabby, mangy hell?

When pig is outcast, darling, all is well.

Sly bastard

All week long Ace tried to write the poem.
Nothing. Worse. Rubbish. Sunday morning
he upped like a man bent on resurrection
and started writing with a watery sun shining

like an old lady recovering from her latest stroke,
right hand paralysed, slowbodied, yet with critical faculty intact.
Ace released his dreamfloods and hoped they'd flow
through-beyond the world of intimidating fact.

But no, there was no light in the words, no glory
in the morning, no angel-echoing of his bones and blood.
Instead, that sly bastard of a poem refused to be written

but lay hidden deep within or way out in space and time
sneering at Ace like an acquisitive, ungiving god
dangling poems like stars beyond the reach of men,

beyond their touch but not beyond their sight,
visible in darkness, lost in light.

Now, I ask you, for a poet, isn't that a miserable fucking plight?

Harmony Street

There is, suddenly, a going beyond
into light and a puzzle never known before
and a resting there
and a return from there
to find things as they were
yet different
because the light on the bridge
tells the story of every stone,
the mockery of one music by another
is a definition of politics
and the voice on the phone
slits Europe open like a pig's throat
to release the blood and provide the meat
that, for one cruel season at least,
will feed the kids in that ravenous house
at the fallingdown end of Harmony Street.

Bit o' sport

Manic black clouds chase a small white cloud
across the sky, this can't be fair,
five greyhounds, murderous crowd,
chasing a hare
in a field in Sallowglen.
Clouds are a lot like men.

Success

While she sang outside
in the long corridor
he was inside
examining photographs
of her as a moist young bride
with a silencing style
the success of which was due
(he was convinced)
to an assiduously practised smile.

The 7B

A darling girl from Clare
got the 7B bus in Dublin,
saw an old woman
sitting alone,
fragile, trembling, grey.

The girl from Clare
studied her.

For the first time in her life, she thought
'One day I'll be grey as that,
my head, my armpits, my cunt
grey, all grey.'

That night she dyed her hair
black as tar and slept
as soundly as before.

When she spoke to Ace
there were red blotches on her neck and face.
Something in her heart was free.

'I declare to God,' she said, 'I'll never be the same again,
the way I think and feel and see.
Something in me changed forever
when I hopped the 7B.'

His praise

Ace spouts hyperbole about her now
she's dead, her brilliant mind, gracious ways.
Why did he never speak of her like this when living?
Why had she to die to earn his praise?

So glad

Ace watched her giving birth.
Afterwards, her heart was so glad
he knew she'd opened like his mind
never had.

Freckles

A freckle between her breasts
A freckle above her left heel;
Ace studied both, mentioned one.
How, she purred, do you think that makes me feel?

On the rocks

The mermaid lay warm on the rocks,
drowsy, not looking about.
'Have you ever been fucked?' asked Cox.
She said 'No.' He said 'You are now.'
'What do you mean?' she asked the old lout
who replied with a smile, 'The tide's out.'

Lift

Ace met her in a lift in Dunne's Stores.
She said he was one of the slitheriest whores
she'd ever met.

       He said, 'You look old.'
'Older than you,' she said, 'and a thousand times more bold.'
She took a low-fat vanilla yoghurt from his bag.
She laughed, a girl.
He spluttered, venomous old hag.

Or just himself in drag?

Plots

Phantoms of forbidden fruit haunt the airwaves.
   Out from Pandora's box
pour ghosts of shining bodies, sweating words,
   dying-for-Ireland cunts and cocks.
Tuck up the bombs. Out with the verbal tricks
   to amuse the suits in originating places.
The stars are children with frightened faces.

The undeniable beauty of denial

Ace asked a Major Political Figure
   why he'd spread
the spewy rumour about his colleague.
'I wanted to hear him deny it,' he said.

The art of public discussion

Two politicians
are barking on the radio.
Neither listens to the other.
Gas fuckin' men, aren't they, ha?

When arse and mouth are one

He squirms beneath contempt and squirms so well
contempt spits in his dandruff, then chooses Hell.
Hell, beneath contempt, craves air. Air is scarce,
so scarce Hell gulps it from the politician's arse.
Hell sickens, vomits in the shivering sun,
the politician's arse and mouth are one.
When he shits, his language stinks the town
and can be heard and smelt for miles around.

Brown shoes

Brown shoes on the floor
brown towel flung on a chair
everyone in that photograph dead and gone
the old house knocked, another in its place
my bag packed and ready to go
where I know nobody, mused Ace.

His head split open.

Outside time again, no blood, just split open.
What a way to see my days,
my work, my attempts at loving.
Such a view of pain, communication.

I want to greet my brothers and sisters everywhere
I want to say how much I think of you all
though I've never met you.
I can only see you
when my head splits open like this
and time is a bundle of old rags pitched in a bin
telling me I have nothing to lose
not even old photographs
not even brown shoes.
From here it seems possible to love each other
to sit at the world's table together
and listen to the stories
we have for each other.
There is something we must understand.
Stories at the table will help us not to kill
or screw each other to death for power and money.
This is coming out of the split in my head
this is the mocking fear of the living
and the authority of the dead
it is, you might say, a mad moment
a moment of beautiful delirium visionary fever
the truest moment I've known for a long time
it cannot last
it is mine forever.

Cargo

Bearing bits of paper, bags and condoms
the hissing Liffey yahoos tonight
seawards with a cargo of our latest scandals.
Listen, love, listen! And hold on tight!

The cries of time

Why Ace left the house in the suburbs
with the woman standing at the door
bidding him farewell, a serious farewell
believing he was going nowhere
since that's what their attempts to live
together proved beyond all doubt to her

will not be stated here, let alone explored
(certain forms of agony leave everybody bored).
But leave he did, to find the Bluebell Pad,
walks by the Liffey of death and love
and rambling chats with Lucifer and God.

Such ramblings! Such wanderlust of mind!
Up and out in the dripping middle of the night,
wandering through the Phoenix Park
that he might contemplate the Dublin light.

Once, as he strolled the midnight gloom
he heard cries he'd never heard before.
His whole world became a tiny room
and all the cries lived in his blood and bones.

Cries of animals he'd heard, cries of birds,
of children, beaten women, hunger-cries,
cries of silent pain, voices on the phone,
cries of girls fucked by lies,
cries of old men ditched in homes for nobody,
cries of women who have seen through men
or haven't, cries of poverty, of money,
cries of lovers knowing love won't come again.

But the cries of time proclaimed themselves the cries of time
and nothing more. How so? It was the way
they cried for all things but themselves,
all hearts, especially those with nothing to say.

Like Ace's heart that night not long ago, or long ago.

Nothing to say. Nor did Ace try to say
anything but shambled through the darkness
till he came to the river shambling to the sea.

What have you to say, river? What have you to say to me?

For a while, again, Ace was ice. How long
in God's name would it take him to melt
back to mankind? That's the beauty of walking
through night, that slow sense of melting without guilt,
the search for weariness, the dream of sleeping
if not in a lover's arms, well then, alone,
the pillow blood-spotted, the dream beginning,
the cries of time trapped in a sleeping man
and who knows the gifts and griefs of morning?

Slice

'I know,' she said, 'when we laugh and fuck
life's a blessèd slice of luck.'

For that

He was, we agreed, the nastiest bastard who'd ever lived
there; a real dickhead, stab-in-the-back rat.
    But he wrote a song we all loved
        and we love him for that.

The problem of smithereens

The day Ace created God he was
a pip of gravel at the back of a rock
hidden away from sunlight and grass
a damp weeping unseen thing

       but he was also, still, a man
   animated by nothingness
who knew the meaning of being cursed
   and blessed.

He could walk the menacing streets
   see the creatures in the shadows
creatures that would live
         when men would be no more.

No more. These newbods are creating
         themselves even now,
they will come to us through
      our minds' windows,
cause us to vanish,
      not be spoken of,

so that we are all without a hereafter,
     a history.

There will have been no past, no mention
of gravel or stones or Christ.

You could say (had you the words) it will
      be new
but there will be no words. No words will do

for one turning creation upside
          down

playing havoc with his own position
exhausting himself to create
his own loneliness,
his infinite kingdom of private blackness
     which he must trust
      or forever be accursed.

I am not at the bottom of the river, thinks Ace,

nor am I
a candidate for moon-travel
or spectacular odysseys into legendary hell.

I am
walking
the streets of Dublin

listening to a scientist
saying how simple it would be

to blow this world to smithereens.

What will happen the smithereens?

Daisy

Daisy stayed one night, one utterance night,
and when she left the old rat died
a while but recovered when he saw
her later, all in white, a bride

beautiful beyond all talk-to-me dirty. 'Twas Eastertide.

Crossing the bridge

When the old lady stopped Ace on O'Connell Bridge
and asked 'What is a poem, Mr de Horner?'
Ace was flummoxed. The old lady went on,
'Whenever I hear or read a poem

I feel as if I'd a friend somewhere
who surprises me in the strangest ways,
I see pictures in my mind which I
haven't seen since childhood days,

I hear music sweet as my father's fiddle
in the house I was born in down the country.
But, Mr de Horner, when I read your twaddle
I'm listening to the squeaks of a lost and lonely

soul. You do have a soul, Mr de Horner,
don't you? Don't you? A soul? In spite of your jingles?'

                              Ace lowered his head.

'A soul,' he murmured, 'A soul...' He trailed off.

'Thank you for telling me all that,' the old lady said

and crossed the bridge into one of the jungles.

Peacock painting

On her left buttock was imprinted
     the head of a man
looking up to heaven, it seemed.
     The man was praying,
she said, in earnest gratitude
because he'd achieved everything
he'd ever dreamed. And
     she added with a smile,
'That was after the peacock screamed.'

That pain

Ace went down
               under a post-colonial kick in the balls.
His screams wreckoed about the town.

O boy, this is history at its worst,
               the poor, dumb, screaming thing
                    doubled-up, accursed.

They could play whatever fiddles they had,
           adore the pure tradition,
impeccably lamenting, flawlessy sad,

dismiss every corrupting alien note
           that Whiteboys and Holy Terrors
might cut some landlord's throat

and prompt a back-o'-the-parish balladeer
           to make an immaculate song.
There was Ace in the gutter,

testicles swelling like pride. Why,
           he daren't even rub them.
A modest caress might be a guilty cry,

the safest thing is to cringe and whine
           in neat yelping poems
tasty as bargain wine.

Therefore, he grieved in the pure tradition.
           It paid off. His balls improved,
sound as a perfect Act of Contrition

muttered to God in the dark, deep and scary.
           Whoever had kicked him had disappeared.
Was the kicker sorry?

Ace was. Very. For what? Had there not been a crime?
           And was he not the victim?
Who would be tried? Who would do time?

What would time do to him in return?
           Ace thought of eternity (or tried to)
till his face, brain and heart began to burn

like a fire started for fun on an August
           Bank-Holiday by a happy gang:
next day, black circle of ashen dust.

He upped from the gutter and walked away
           towards Bluebell and history.
That pain guaranteed he had something to say

which, though not pure, might live in its own way.
'Twould be fun, would it not, to knock a kick
                    out of agony,

transfigure withering moments of shame
                to the point where he'd say that a kind
of laughing dignity is the name of the game.

Ace staged himself

Hearing the cries, the cries,
Ace staged himself, tragic clown,
took a seat in the lower gods,
became a critic, watched himself
till the curtain came down.

His critique was savage, the final
sentence ('most foolish of writers
fails to portray saddest of men'),
a knife in his heart.

Try again. His brain continued
to stage itself as he shuffled
through wind and rain.

So many plays fell out of his head
on to the pavement
he began to feel more alive than dead,
to enjoy himself again
and so to know what the grave meant.

He made magical small theatres
out of cups of coffee
and invited the world to see his plays,
to sip their magic.

The world came, tasted, went away
scratching its head, a touchy, wise,
let-me-think look in its eyes.

For a surprising number of days
this enabled our tragic clown
to live with his cries, his cries,
to upstage himself when he was down,

a talent that earned him a certain fame
in the adjudicating town.

Miracles

Miracles are common enough in Dublin,
    the greatest, a day without hurt.
No miracle, though, if you walk on the Liffey.
    That beauty is solid with dirt.

Knock

'When did I last see my vagina?' she wondered, standing
    naked on the bedroom floor.
Her body tensed like the salmon of knowledge
    at the knock on the door.

The Mistake

'My mother told me I came arse-first into the world'
said the swag-bellied man to Ace.
'She told me my birth had not been planned.
From the start, sir, my path was treacherous,

slippery always. My mother was an honest woman,
her candour was exemplary, she said she
found it hard to see me as entirely human
and that she'd never wanted me.

What could I do, faced with such integrity?
She was the most intrepid woman I've ever known.
She called me the Mistake.

It's what I am: a loony faculty,
error of judgement, a thing gone wrong,
a failed abortion on the make.'

Ace looked the Mistake straight in the eyes:
a man incapable of lies.

What it must feel like

'I never did anything right in my life,' said the Mistake.
'If I try to write a poem or a song
the final concoction will seem to most folk
almost blasphemously wrong.

And when I try to love a woman
with what I take to be my heart
she cocks her snout at me as though I were
a bottled fart.

For weeks, then, I hide. I hide. I emerge,
enter a shop, buy a book, proceed to read,
finish the thing. Yet when I try to speak
of it, that bloody book has betrayed my head.

'I often wonder,' said the Mistake, 'as I lie awake at night
what it must feel like to do something right.'

The heart of the matter

The Mistake was also known as Arsefirst because
of his style of entry into this world.
Once, he named himself Arsefirst the First
but dropped the title since it imperilled

his safety at home and abroad
and made him feel like an oil-slick on our coast
forcing a thousand people, working night
and day at considerable cost

to themselves, to purge the country of him.
Oil-slick! Thick, black, stupid, awful – his heart,
the heart of the matter of the Mistake

or Arsefirst, as you will. Neither land nor sea
wanted him. How could he play his part?
How could he give? Who'd bother to take?
Who'd honour him with a humble place?

Arsefirst asked these questions, hid his face.

Divorce

I must get myself right, dreamed the Mistake,
I don't want to be an error forever,
I've got to rectify myself, somehow,
shake off this state of dull, implacable terror

invading my gut, poor gut, anonymous
and winding through my inner territory
where I wander, lost and pusillanimous.
How does a mistake stop being a mistake?

The Mistake exploited his capacity for dreaming.
In his dream he encountered his mother
Betsy, who'd christened him The Mistake.

The Mistake filed for divorce from nasty Betsy.
He succeeded, the first Irishman to divorce
his mother. He was drunk for a week.

Everyone said he was up the fuckin' creek.

Alone and in the company

It's not so much, thought Ace, that I see myself as phoney,
shrewdly worthless, a glib, articulate sham,
        it's rather
that I know myself by knowing, now and then,
alone
and in the company of other men
        how small,
how infinitely small I am.

No wonder I don't give a damn.

A consequence of good fortune

A Dublin woman won the Lotto.
   Ever after, in the pub,
she'd order two drinks,
sip one herself
and pour the other down her knickers.
When asked by a fascinated bystander
what in God's name
she'd do a thing like that for
she replied
'It's a mean, mean world, brother.
There's only one cunt
I'll buy a drink for!'

What does drunk mean anyway?

The city stumbles, falls flat on its face.
de Horner sings wet laneways of disgrace.

Fleabag Muldowney homes at his own pace.
God bless all this embottled race.

A shadow

Climbing Folklore Hill one sunny morning
Ace was nearly happy. Then a shadow
darkened a green railing and he thought
of someone he'd love to kill.

No lies

Bullets spray
the children's bedroom
as if one of them
in a fit of temper
flung marbles
at the walls. The holes
open, like sick eyes.
Marina is crying.
Jenny is starving.
Deirdre seems sleeping.
The holes are no lies.

The jobless die young

The old have worked to make it.
                Let them sing their song.
            The jobless die young
                    and
                    there
                    are
three hundred thousand such, at least,
            on this battered rock
                    plonked
in the frantic Atlantic, northwest

of Europe, Ace mumbled to nobody
because nobody was listening and

                who cared?

Effect of nothing

'There's nothing out there,' he said
            'nothing with the power
            to love or forgive.'

'What is the effect of nothing on you?'

            'I want to live.'

Pit of the Joy

Twelve rapists co-shackle in a pit of the Joy.
One has curly black hair, moves
       like a rippling athletic boy,
nothing at all in his face to indicate how,
       one stalking night,
he dragged Angela Barr down a laneway
       and extinguished her light.

How the resolute soul is shaken

Samantha Beckett resolved never to smile again.
She'd had enough of showing the teeth, gums
(sometimes) lips opening (in pain?)
breath escaping freely, a stink of slums

in summer, heat weakening all but the best-fed,
liver and gizzard protesting as well,
not to mention the arch dizziness of the head
recalling tales of such mayhem one thinks of hell.

       Maybe that's what Samantha thought of too.

In any case, from now on, the smile was out,
thing of the past, corpsed, buried in style.

      Walking down Grafton Street
         she met, out of the blue,
an old pal from whose assiduous mouth
           foul yarns were wont to sprout.
          He told one now.
          Samantha listened.
          Couldn't help it.
          Smile.

Nothing like funny filth to shake the resolute soul.
Of which puke-stocking art, Dublin is the Capital.

So far

Not much escapes Samantha Beckett.
She has a passion for killing rats
(God help us, God help the rats) and she
has explored every make of rat-trap known to man
to help her in this dark activity.

Extermination is Samantha's thing
because she swears the rats are killing
language, ritual and fun.

Something must be done!

Therefore, she has ways to seize rats by the ears
claws tails and dump them, dead, in
the Liffey,
grave of rats and drunken culchies
out of money, home and work, fed-up with not
being fed, so Liffeymud's the answer, mate.

Samantha, on the Halfpenny Bridge, stares in the river's
assorted poisons and thinks of every rat
that has escaped her so far. So far. Remember that.

A tip

Whenever Ace meets Samantha Beckett
she sweeps him off his cornpadded feet.
She smiles and shines and says 'O feck it,
let's go to the Curragh for the race-meeting

this afternoon. I've a tip that's bound to come
up and you look like you need a trip
out of yourself, you're locked in that cage, old son,
so get yourself together and quit this kip

of a city for a whack o' the Kildare crack.
I was born in Foxrock meself and I know
what squinting hells these villages can be.'

Ace winces, pretends he has a pain in his back,
says he loves the thought but cannot go.
Samantha smiles, shines, heads for the Curragh, free.

The Golden Calf

Last year, the Franco-Anglo-Foxrock Competition
            was for a song or verse
portraying despair, angst or that sense of perdition
            which simply cannot get worse
no matter how shat-on the sufferer may be
            in this wistfully defecating town.
The prize was a Golden Calf, especially
            carved by a genius in London.

Samantha Beckett composed a song of despair
that made stones and several critics weep.
She won the Golden Calf.

Ace de Horner met Samantha somewhere
near Bluebell. 'Why did you write it?' he asked.
'For a laugh, darling,' chuckled Samantha, 'for one hell of a laugh.'

Non Smoking Area

'You kill rats, Samantha' I said, 'You gamble on horses,
            you write prize-winning songs of despair
            yet you tend to giggle, chuckle, laugh. Why?'

'If I didn't kill rats, I'd kill men,' she replied.
            'If I didn't gamble, I'd rot with caution
            and if I didn't laugh, I'd cry.'

'You're one shockin' puzzle of a woman, Samantha,' I said.
'You're a bit of a crossword yourself,' she smiled.

'Will we solve each other yet?' I asked.
'Solutions appear in the papers,' she laughed

and hit for the Galway Races
to bet on a fifty-to-one shot
called *Dún Laoghaire Andotherplaces.*

Who said Four?

I haven't been there so how can I know?
I've been there and I know
Mother Redcap couples in May.

Samantha Beckett dances all night
and doesn't care who knows it.
I think Samantha's right.

How'll I build confidence from here on in?
What'll I do with the body?
Slag the bastard, get to know it as never before,
introduce it to the Four Roynish Truths.
Who said Four?
If I try one, and like it, I may want a score.

A bit of white paper

That October day was more beautiful
than any the summer had given.
Ace delighted in the unpredictable
magnanimity of heaven.

That evening, he saw a magpie screechbully a raven
over a bit of white paper
drifting here and there
and nowhere.

Next morning was ten people dead,
massacred: men, women, children.
A bit of white paper. Bomb. Magpie. Raven.
All buried in his graveyard head.

Stitch

The men took
Christ the knife
and cut Ireland
in two.

What will stitch me?
Ireland cried.
The men replied
'murder will do.'

Aceprayer

Dear God,

Please help me to be less of a shit
to myself and others,
to others and myself, I mean.
Let me not pretend to wisdom and wit
beyond my reach.
Let me try to keep the lies
out of my scribbling
and my life.
I'd like to understand
the hearts of killers rapists bombers,
skilled murderers of happy moments,
I'd like to be the best slogger
I'm capable of being,

I'd dearly like never to become
(maybe I am already)
a self-important bollocks
if only because of the offence
to my sense of perspective
such as it is.
Give me a sense of humour
that I may endure myself
and the world which also
endures me
and the way I try to see.
Let me love the sea
and the contribution made to it
by the sniffy Liffey
of my dreams and longings,
itchy nights and days
that continue to amaze me.
Please help me to keep
the termless threat of boredom
to a minimum
and if it comes
like a disease from
outside history
give me the coppernossity
to do a dance in Bluebell
or Stoneybatter
or any available street
where Vikings walk
and Normans talk
and Dubliners drink and prattle.
When I greet
friends and cherished enemies
let me mean it.
Hello, I say, hello
and how's the body today?
What if each response be circumspect?
Let me learn to respect the way
I despise myself at times,
let me be kind
without thinking,
let me enjoy these old streets
of angels and demons
gambling and drinking
playing it safe
gossiping
till the monuments are blue in the face.

Let me catch the poems as they come
like rain or snowflakes
or devils in dreams
or shouts from a pub
or screams from the darkness
or letters from strangers
or whispers in bed.
When I'm down let me fight
till I'm real to myself again
and to women and men
trying to be free
of what would imprison me
should I give in.
Let me see truly
listen patiently
hear clearly
smell accurately
touch lovingly.
May I embody and emspirit
one tenth of a millionth
of a billionth of a smidgeon
of grace.
      And give me, please,
        good health
or as much of it
as will keep me
ticking over and my
heart in the right place
wherever that is.

      Yours hopefully,
       Ace

Voice among the flowers

The most beautiful model in Dublin
is goddessing down Grafton Street
in her floatingly elegant way.
Ace hears a voice among the flowers:
    'Ya'd never tink, wudya,
      that the same lady loves
  to shite three times a day?'

A bright man

'I could sit here forever
thinking of the day I nearly killed my brother.
He mocked me. When he repeated
these words, I threw a hammer at his head
and missed, barely. My brother said
'O Christ!'
My brother is a bright man.
He never mocked me again.'

He was dead

He was dead, he came to me in sleep,
his eyes were tired and wise, he said
'It's just as trivial here as there.
I hope you're enjoying paradise.'

Alarm

Near midnight, the alarm sounded,
continued all night.
Ace, robbed of his dreams,
had no one to appeal to.

All night the alarm insisted,
exiled sleep to the North Pole
where it lay in white acres of ice,
watchful

as Ace sat alone and listened
to warnings the darkness laughed at
because so many crimes were going on
nobody bothered about.

Who is warning whom? What's wrong?
Is there a thief, murdered at the door?
Where did it originate? To whom does it belong?
Will it go on forever?

It's his brain now, his brain needs it like blood,
craving every shrieksound to the last drop.
Whatever lives are chopped tonight, dear God,
this must never stop.

Bench

Why is my heart a haunted house
Ace asked himself one April night
haunted by a ghost who lives in me?

Why sit on this bench in dying light
afraid I'll be accosted by some curious
human who'll stare at me and see

what a living ghost may do to one?
Give me this empty Park, myself alone,
her ghost turning my heart to stone

or to every envenomed trafficspit in this town.

How many such weepies have sat on that bench
and would still, if it came to the crunch?

Heads

Ace walked down Dame Street.
A man approached, head-butted
the poet in the face.
Dazed, Ace mumbled
            'Whatcha do that for?'
'You owe me forty quid,' the man said.

'Never saw you before in my life,' grumbled Ace.
'Christ you're right,' the man said
and walked off.
Ace shook his head
and dizzied on, aware
he'd never seen the man before.
Would he ever see him again?
Alone in Dame Street, anything can happen.
The heart of Dublin ticks like a bomb in the garden.

Counter attack

'Has the pride of Irish whiskey come to this?
I'd be better off drinkin' Parnell's piss!'

A long and revered tradition of Irish hospitality

Ace drank all night, bottling farther and farther
    from others. He found his host and said
        'You're a fucking wanker!
            Piss off to bed!'

Before a word may be written

Look at the drugs, the druggies, carriers, buyers, sellers
drinkers, pissers, hitmen, begrudgers, spoofers, wasters, chancers.
Question the day, the hour, waves of seas and streetcorners,
right, wrong. Then question the questions that spawned the answers.

Historicity

Who killed Carmody? Who threw his coat in the Liffey?
What does his name signify in that appalling song?
    Don't ask Ace, he wasn't there, and if he
were, he'd probably have got it wrong.

Sniggers

He sniggers, his mouth a cancerhole.
Predictable venom slits his eyes.
Sniggers attend the wake and funeral
when reputation dies.

Dirt

            When Ace looks in the dirt
of a pub floor, a street, some grotty place,
he sees, dimly at first, then clearly,
a grieving, handsome face.

He stares into the dirt, more
privileged now than he's ever been.
The face appears, fades, appears again.
The dirt makes Ace a new man.

I could live there, he thinks, I could live
contemplating that face
more beautiful and sorrowful than any
it has been my joy to witness.

Yet I know men who'd kick it to death
some Saturday night in O'Connell Street,
kick in the eyes, cheekbones, forehead, skull,
then lurch away, and forget

or seem to forget, not mentioning it when
they meet in a suburb of hell
and get drunk together, watchful still,
in the bar of the Angel Hotel.

If I look closely now, thinks Ace, I'll see
the men's faces become that face
handsome and grieving still, still framed in the dirt,
metamorphosis.

The murderers of the face have entered the face,
live there, waiting to be seen
by Ace and his ilk alive to possible grace
in the killing town

where kickers-to-death of strangers go lost
and free, giving no sign
that any streetwalker might think their faces
are other than yours or mine.

A tricky art

Ace listened to the poet readingbleeding in public
relishing the measured shedding
of each drop of his blood. He struck
a shivery note with a poem about his wedding
and the sad disintegration of his best
intentions.

   Then came a heartscalding lyric
about the necessary dumping of his beloved
children.

   Verse is so savage it makes you sick
but you recover, injected with the sheer music
of the thing.

The most touching poem of all
dramatised the poet's need to survive
himself, then others; this involved destruction, shock
decisions, back-stabbing, arse-licking, betrayal,
a bumpy circus-ride through good and evil.

He ended the reading with a neat song of love.

Moping home through the rhythmical night
Ace pondered the transformation of emotional shite,
a tricky art when almost all is said and done
in Dublin London Tokyo Belfast Bluebell Babylon.

Starlight Clohessy on philosophy

'Aristotle makes me witty
Plato makes me wise
but what do I care for their philosophy
with your prick between my thighs?'

All the way

Ace saw a woman on O'Connell Bridge.
        She saw him too.
          They stood.
   'What's your name?' he asked.
'Janey Mary,' she replied,
      'but if you're in a hurry
        Janey will do.
   And who are you?'

'Ace,' he intoned, 'Ace de Horner,' letting the syllables roll.

'Ace,' she murmured, 'Ace and Janey Mary.'
   Then, 'Would you like to go for a stroll?'

'Right y'are,' he answered, 'may we head for the Greally Hole?'

   I'm with you all the way, said Janey Mary's smile.

2

A question without an answer,
an answer without a question.

A change of heart, at what price?

A valororous, fat, sozzled, brown-headed woman
accosts Ace outside the Shelbourne Hotel,
asks him for money. He refuses.
She wishes him to the floor of hell.

He hands her some cash, sighing 'Oh well!'

Her fist closes. She smiles. The floor of hell
is preferable to her smile.

The things she comes out with

    First morning kiss:
  Janey Mary stretched and said
(as if to the cheeky light flirting with her head)
'I'll be like the flight of the bumble-bee after this!'

Penny

'What the hell use is poetry to anyone or anything?
Why persist in bullshitting about the dark night
of the soul? What is your purpose, man, what
is your purpose?'
                    Ace was dumb,
the economist kicked him in the guts and spine
and told him to study money.
                    Ace crawled home
and studied a penny
   bright and shiny
undulled as yet by the fingers of men,
   very small like Ace's self-esteem.

The penny made him remember himself as a child
when a penny was fun, infinite fun.

He remembered two pennies covering a corpse's eyes,
men praising the corpse when alive.
He saw pennies drop into an outstretched hand,
words of blessing rise, clear and sweet
beyond the world of beggary, loss, lies,
into the surviving skies.
He saw pennies on the side of a street,
himself and others playing pitch-and-toss.
Where were they now? He began to brood
on the loss of friends, the loss
of pictures in his shat-on head:

Matthew Farth who lost every tittle o' sense
thanks to his martyr's obsession with women;
Dabbler Coote who spent long years
finishing a never-finished self-portrait;
Fisher Lynch who spent his nights
poaching salmon in rivers and lakes;
Maggie Denny who lived in a caravan
and filled it with flowers for Saint Martha.

Where were they now? Ace
pressed the penny against his face
and smiled.

       The smile eased his pain.
There was nothing to explain
with pictures like that for company.
He smiled at the pictures. He was free
as he dared to be,

and grateful for a penny.

Shining

When False God shines into a room
no one is bored or boring.
Everyone in the place looks up,
adoring.
False God acknowledges all this with a smile,
eyes speculatively whoring.

Where it's happening

'Bookworm,' she laughed, 'that's a funny word.
I don't read books, neither do me pals,
books are slow, too slow,
books are for old people.
I like videos instead.
Videos are where it's happening, man,
videos open up my head
so I can see
weird planets splitting you and me.'

(So the rumour goes)

The city of Dublin is founded
on rumour and mud.
The mud (so the rumour goes)
is surprisingly clean.

Am I a clown in a circus
that no longer exists?

Or is this how the circus has always been?

A few doors away

A woman who survived Auschwicz lives
   a few doors away from Ace.
Her Dutch husband left her after the war.
   Ace loves to listen to her.
He has never met anyone who more loves
   the smell of wet grass
or the sight and sound of a child
   raising one hell of a stir.

Uses of murder

Atlantic breakers stormbomb the Cashen shore.
A fly writhes, tortured in summer tar.
Today's terrorist is tomorrow's Minister
for varied and fruitful are the uses of murder.

Above the chimney-pot

universes of truth
undreamed-of laws
beyond anything suggested
in Plato Shakespeare Einstein
and Kanooce's jaws

stretch

Brink

Not for the first time Ace tottered to the brink
of himself. Why did he choose to try to live?
Because a voice told him not to give
a fuck about what people think.
Whatever caused his mind to freeze and burn
told him this was what he had to learn
and never forget

though he may, yet.

Predator

He waits for the marked man to emerge
from the house in that leafy part of the city.
The man comes out, the predator converges,
the man is troubled, pale, trembling slightly,
his eyes more hurt than anyone's
the predator has seen on his revealing travels.

Time for questions.

The predator hurls them like balls,
stones, cudgels, sticks, knives. The man
stammers, doesn't break, tries to answer
in a voice beaten, truthful and weary
speaking of his own and other people's lives.
The predator takes notes, the man leaves, the predator
smiles at millions wolfing his exclusive story
bound to bring a thrill
to souls coping with a Sunday morning hell.

Sources?

Is it evil in his eyes
stole lines from Paradise?
When pitbulls face each other in a Finglas pit
what commandment governs that?

Pilgrim souls

'When you,' said Ace to Janey Mary
    'are old and grey
I shall streefle your goodles at night
    and sometimes during the day.'

'And I,' rippled Janey Mary 'shall bounce
    your blind old carcase off the wall
for fun, pure fun, 'cos I never once
    had a teddybear when I was small.'

Junglespeak

Ace likes one poem of his own; it deals
    with the struggle to grow young
and is written on paper made
    from recycled elephant dung.

Originality

'Lie still,' she said, 'lie still and let me hear
   that poem about Original Sin.
Lie still and feel me suck the truth
   out through your withering skin.'

Meetings

'When and where did we meet?' he asked.
   'God only knows,' she said
        'But when you love me
          you explore
forgotten strangers in your bed.'

Down to heaven went her head.

His heart began to sing
listening
to strangers in every corner of his being,
whispering, accusing, affirming.

A moral indignator

'She'll not make me her whore's apprentice.
I wouldn't fuck her for practice.
That ugly bitch should be jailed.'

When Ace heard that he was glad to know
tiger's semen can now be frozen
though all attempts at artificial insemination have failed.

September, 1991

Abortions? Go to hell
or England. While women weep and bleed
the lads are feeling fit and well
climbing the mountains of their greed.

Ace yawps the gob, gulps the bad seed
reading a politician who, he knows,
wouldn't give his shit to the crows.

A Young Wife's Tale

'Up with it
in with it
and may the Lord have his will with it.'

Some nights

'Some nights I lie awake and watch you,' said Janey Mary,
'and it's like watching a dog dreaming.
I don't really know what
the dreams are about
as they bang and clatter in the dark
        but now and then you excite me
        with your quivering body,
        with your dreaming dog's
        muffled bark.'

Drowning

There's a rainbow forming
this wet September evening
over Dublin. A seagull
settles on wet slate.

If I understand you, will it be too late?

I've never been much use at knowing
what's going on in people's hearts and heads,
the kind of darkness I drown in
rather than understand.
Your words are luminous and beautiful.
I wish I had the courage to drown in them
or let them take me by the hand
and lead me wherever they've a mind to go,
          undiscovered roads
          hugger-mugger lanes
             streets of vertigo.

The Good News

I told him I was getting married.
His lip
curled into a question:
'Will she take the whip?'

Doorway

A woman shouts obscenity at the doorway.
Love is worded, praise is given.
The darkest secrets of the heart
are broad daylight in heaven.

Best bit

'Did he pull down her panties or push 'em aside?
Did he rape her? Did she lead him on?
Did he half-throttle her?
Did she give him that scar? O man dear,
it's the best bit o' telly I seen
since the Gulf War.'

The struggle for equality

Witchmouth, choice perfume, nose
sharper by the hour, smile
clean as a bullet:
fucks her way to power.

Gives me the scour.

But who am I?
Jealous bastard, really.

In there, in there, where Ace cannot see
is where I long to be.

Three doors

You went through the yellow door.
I followed, picking
flowers from your laughter.

You walked through the green door.
I watched you comb your long hair
in front of the fire.

You walked through the white door.
Home is the best place
to know a stranger.

Three doors in my mind tonight:
yellow, green, white.
I'll open them all, enter,
stand, look, follow
the pictures in the pitiless light.
The doors will close behind me, each one
a loved, lost thought of you
whom I never knew
or allowed to know me.
Where am I now?
Walking away from the doors
to the place of no doors,
the place
where I'll meet hell in many a face
and not feel too bad about it.

Is it the most hellish thing of all
that one can get used to anything?
That every door is there to be opened
revealing pictures
leading to nothing?

There

A poor village
at the back-end of nowhere,
people working hard,
no ideas, no sophistication.
It happened there.

When word reached us, we turned it
into something else. I ask you
how could it possibly have remained
what it was in the beginning,
in that nowhere place?
It had to change.

There'll be a million versions from now on.
You have yours.
I have mine.
But Christ in heaven,
wait'll it hits the small screen!

Poor Ace works hard
trying to define
the obscene.

Reading lesson

When the green demons insist 'You matter'
Ace reads the Dublin gutter
and finds what can't be written on paper.

Fable

The ditched paper clipped his left ankle.
The tied bicycle's front wheel was missing.
A boy grabbed a purse from an old woman
who cursed him, fleeing...

      Ace saw it all, wondered
  (no, the thought hit him, from nowhere)
Can I imagine what it's like
      to have no being.

      no being?

The ditched paper danced along the pavement.
A girl in a green coat looked at him,
laughing, trembling a little, laughing.

He shrank into himself. Nothing.
Or a fable
he would tell himself
when the predictable flesh grew feeble.

Yet the flesh would listen
as it always did
and make of the fable
whatever it could

      and follow the lines of light
      and decipher its words
      and live with its echoes
         turning
      to raindrops on his window
      love-abuse on Janey Mary's lips

children's cries in the street
keys turning in doors
vivid pieces of dreams

the perfect no-ending to a story
forever incomplete

Screaming streets

Ace turned a corner
  in a mucky city street,
      saw love
  begging in the rain,
blue fingers gripping a white bowl
  darkness coming on
  like one hell of a question.

'I love you,' he said.

Seconds were centuries.

'I know,' love replied.

Old streets were screaming that he lied.

From the street

'Janet never faces up to her feelings
though she's outrageous, beautiful and bright.
The day her father died she picked a stranger
from the street, and fucked all night.

Fucking is pure escape, she says, and laughs in sad delight.'

She and the machine

Isn't it bloody gas!

She did a fair old Leaving Cert,
got into Trinity
slept with every don
she could lay her hands on
or throw the leg across.

In 1994
the Business Studies Studs
(with an eye on Political Science)
voted her
FUCK OF THE YEAR.

I saw it with my own eyes
written on a door
in a loo in the third floor
of the Arts Block.

How could that be wrong?

Nothing she wouldn't do for money,
no pill
she wouldn't swallow.
More pricks went up that woman
than pikes up Vinegar Hill.

Then she took to going abroad,
Paris, Rome, Berlin, Madrid.
When she hit these places
I leave it up to yourself to imagine
what she did.

Imagine what she did!

God!

And of course it had to happpen:
AIDS.

I saw her in Davy Byrne's last night
knockin' back the gin
as if she were
the healthiest woman in Dublin.

Poxy, rotten bitch!

Stay clear of her!
Clear!

You were warned. Remember.

How long has she to go?

Not long, so far as I know.

Better dead
than in bed, say I, says he, say we.

> *Somewhere in Bluebell*
> *she walks alone*
> *enjoying the air,*
> *enjoying the way*
> *the cool September breeze*
> *plays through her hair*
>
> *while she moves towards the Liffey*
> *as if she didn't care,*
>
> *as if she didn't care.*

Poverty

Ace foraged from an early age,
sometimes following
often rejecting
the advice of his elders.
He saw one cliff
cast a thousand shadows,
one tide embark
on a gifting spree,
laughed with a woman
who'd twenty-two children
('my husband makes
a mattress o' me'),
sang songs that assumed
fifty different versions,
relaxed in wonder
when he heard a hare cry
in the grass and bleed
like a tortured soul;
that's why he agreed
the mouse that knows
one hole alone
is poor indeed.

Design

Ace's first teacher
Mr Matt Battie
a former theologian
held that God
had so designed
human buttocks
they could be lashed
without serious injury.

Bad winters ahead
he must endure
buttocks freezing
in pitiless air
Ace thought of
his old teacher
now resting
in the bosom of his Maker.

Ace winced
at what went on
in his own mind
and wondered how
can your average
man's thoughts be
so savagely unkind.

Quietly, unseen
in the downing town
he rubbed his buttocks
hither and thither
up and down
gently lovingly
and made his way
as best he could
through the world
of unflappable
buttock-designing God.

Education

'How sure and steady is the way?'
'Give him to the Jesuits and you'll see
Why, when a dog is tied down early,
He'll never bother to cut free.'

Underworld

under Dublin streets tonight
parched rats sip freezing water
by sewerlight

Not so bad

'When the great wave of love breaks over the world
we will drown in God.' Ace steps
into the incoming tide, feeling foolish and bad
and sane and lost because his God is mad.
If the tide brought a mermaid, and she were willing
and he able, Ace would be game to ride.
God and the sea have their rhythms. So has this lad.
When the ancient rhythm comes right, he's not so bad.

The necessary step

It was something Ace had to take.
He fiddled, faddled, doodled, dawdled,
wrote a note to an old teacher
for advice, no reply, the teacher's awful

arthritis was grinding him down,
Ace phoned a former lover, she said
he sounded like a truly bolloxed man,
joked about his little willie, how dead

was it now she wanted to know, he hung up
and went for a long walk by the Liffey
seeking a shot of jizz, an injection of pep
which was exactly what he found in a crumbling shop.

Relaxing into a cup of tarblack coffee
he decided to take the necessary step.

A constant friend

Sipping her café au lait
she looks healthy,
talks of her depression:
'If there was a simple way of doing it
I wouldn't be here today.'

Ace thinks of his suicidal nights,
says nothing. Pain is a constant friend,
will be to the end.
He looks into her eyes,
thanking God she's alive.
'You said you'd ring me,' she smiles
'and you did not.'
Ace is cornered, so he lies.
She knows that; and if her smile
is forgiveness, why then the man's forgiven.
'Come on,' she laughs, 'we didn't do it,
we're here, alive and well.
So ring me.'
                    He smiles, half-smiles.
'I will,' he says, 'I will.'

Question to a rolled-over poet

Janey Mary rolled him over on the grass.
'Put me,' she laughed, 'as they say in the Bible, with child.
What would you do, you tame old kiss-me-ass,
If I weren't wild?'

Footnote

that freezing saturday morning
   ace found
a stray child and a stray bomb
   in the london underground

A laneway off Thomas Street

Too tired to dream, Ace took a poem for a walk.
It was a pleasant stroll until they came
to a laneway off Thomas Street.
The poem suddenly bolted and ran away.
Ace never saw it again.
Back in his pad he began to dream
of a robber having fun
with *Twenty Things You Need To Know*
About Prince Andrew
before you're anyone.
The robber conned these things by heart
and decided he'd perfect the art of hit-and-run.
One day he met Ace's poem
gone all astray.
He hit it on the head and ran away
with several of its secrets
which he keeps at home in plastic jars.
Sometimes he lets them out for fresh air
or even a stroll
but back into the jars they go,
little things, winking secrets, fragments,
stolen bits and pieces of Ace de Horner's soul,
hardly worth your time to know.
And if you knew
would you tell Prince Andrew?

Play

Some who play with words may never know
how words may play with them.
Once, in a state of almost-vertigo,
Ace tussled with words in a style changing to dream

of Christmas Eve in Hartford, Connecticut
where lights were dancing on the edge of time.
O such a dance it was de Horner thought
he must join in. He did, and was struck dumb

and motionless as though he'd never been.
The lights had changed to words, each word
an accusation he couldn't answer.

The words mocked, 'Come play with me, sad man,'
but Ace's guilt encaged him. He barely stirred.
He stared at every word changed to a torture-dancer.

The only, the only

I have lived, have I lived, how do I know, Ace mused
as he listened to the pictures talking
in the National Gallery,
I have spoken, been spoken to, spun
a yarn or two, rejoiced in being
victim and propagator of yarns, sung
songs I've forgotten, how much is that doggy
in the window, buddy can you spare a dime,
and now that I'm in my fiftieth year or
thereabouts, can I recall
three sentences, two sentences, one sentence
I have uttered, I say uttered
in all that time?
Can I remember
one word I spoke
during all these babbling decades
to my dead father, dead mother, dead friends?

And my dear lady wife
who once endured me,
what did I say to her?

Ace smiled, shivered, smiled. At that
moment, not a syllable
could he remember.

Not a syllable, just a sense
of small, comic catastrophes
squatting somewhere in his head
like a row of smartass satanists
mocking his language, God help it,
poor scrowly thing that it is
but the only, the only.
And what appallingly forgettable words
hide like assassins
behind walls and hedges of the future?

Ace scratched his head, blinked at the sun
and thanked heaven for oblivion.

Later on

One night, dreaming down the Hill of the Goats,
Ace saw the land melting, the sea advancing
like a rent-collector determined to get his due,
not to accept any excuses
no matter how heart-rending or creative.
With an efficiency unknown in the higher
reaches of the Civil Service, the sea
did its job so that in no time at all
Ace was walking on water, a talent
he'd never suspected he possessed.
Well, what could he do? There wasn't a root
of land left in the world, not a blade of grass,
not a hedge, hill, mountain, valley, glen,
nothing but the sea, reclaiming all these strayed
women and men. Under the moon, Ace sank
back where he belonged and looked around.
He'd have stories, later on, stories
about the astounding world he found.

An inexplicable desire

Shortly after something happened (G'wan! Tell us!)
        Ace began to bite women
                out of an inexplicable desire
                        to avenge himself

on what he daren't begin to understand.
        He'd be sitting there
                in the corner of a pub
                        chatting with Janey Mary

when he'd suddenly bite that healing lady
        in the breast, wrist or throat.
                Needless to say, this got
                      Janey Mary's goat

and she'd thump the malignant ferrety bastard
        with spontaneous gusto
                screaming at him the while
                    'You fucking weirdo!'

Ace would mumble an apology and say
        he didn't really understand
                why he'd done such a thing.
Janey Mary would take him by the hand,

lead him forth into the Dublin night
        along the streets, down a dark lane
                where she'd back him up against a wall
and in her priceless style cause him some pain

which disgraced Ace bore with a loaded groan.
        Was this pleasure? Was it fun?
There in the dark, Janey Mary came
        into her own. She changed her man.

Not that Ace ever shed the desire to bite women
        but he got it under control
                up to a point, anyway.
And isn't that what civilisation is all

about? A bitten woman will change the world
        as Ace de Horner found to his cost.
He also found that certain impulses must be endlessly rediscovered
        and others, lost.

For this moment

For this moment by the river
    of seagull swoop and cry
Ace de Horner is a man
    to whom no adjectives apply.

Letter

February frost: Dublin
is a lost
white letter from a friend
strayed beyond the freezing sea.

By fire and quayside

How was I to know the sadness would return
to numb my body, drown my mind
when you stood by the fire after twenty years
and laughed, and spoke words near and kind
as the woman's by the quayside when she said
'Bit o' love, love? Now. Twenty quid.'

Children of God

The girl kneels, receives God's body and blood
        while at her back
men, their green bags ordained by money,
        stalk.

Home and away

Ace is living me today.
He's at home now, I've slipped away.
Who is saying whatever there's to say?
Who dares shape the curse? Who dares pray?

Cover-up

And who are you this morning, twinkles Ace,
My friend enemy confessor analyst mauler liarlover?
Don't worry, Ace, I say, if this should ever take shape
Some name we recognise will grace/disgrace the cover.

Flexi-time

My guilt complex is on flexi-time.
You might catch me at three in the morning
looking like an alpha graduate from our leading university
of crime,
you know the look, a glare of diabolic warning
in the reddened eyes, the mouth whimpering
to the heart (or vice versa), 'Do you despise me?'
and again, 'Why is your anger lashing me?'
Self-flagellating questions pour incessantly
out of what I presume is my childhood,
boyhood, manhood and whatever hood I'm wearing now,
Spring, the rebellious stretch in the days,
light stalking my eyes like a wee reminder from God
that I should lift my guilt complex out of my heart,
examine it, polish it, absorb it in a thousand new accusing ways.

Big bugger

'I admire the way you speak your heart.
You say exactly what's in your head.
You anger important people. I can't do that.
Big bugger of a mortgage,' he said.

Poems are cheeky bastards

You can use any damned word in a poem
            said Janey Mary.
You can say shit fuck cunt prick and
            get away with it.
Now if I said prick cunt fuck shit, people
            would look at me and think
Jesus, isn't she the vulgar bitch with a tongue
            on her like a slurry-pit.
Why, when the same words appear in a poem
    do people enjoy them like their own farts?
            Why is the poem not guilty?
What's all this tyrannical crap about art?
A prick is a prick, a fuck is a fuck, a cunt
is a cunt, a shit is a shit,
and that's true in and out of a poem
    but one is vulgar, th' other is wit
or wisdom or whatever the poem says it is.

        Poems are cheeky bastards,
            they tickle my heart and head,
they break all the rules and live by their own
            like a night of love, she said.

Morning gravy

She said she'd stayed awake all night
looking at him.
She said he was gentle and soft
and remarkably hairless.
She added he'd slept like a baby.
He mapped his head between her legs
and lapped his morning gravy.

Conversation with an eggshell

Ace sat at table, his eyes
fixed on the remains of breakfast,
a cracked eggshell. For a while,
he contemplated it, fragile yet exquisite
in its way. Then he began to talk to it.
            'Dear eggshell,' he said,
'I too feel cracked and fragile.
Therefore I thank you for reminding me
how important is my style of survival.
The hero-light once filled my eyes, my mind,
and may again, but you are all emptied
of your goodness.
Dear eggshell, what remains for you to do?
Get stuck in a plastic bag
and be dumped somewhere?
Be trodden underfoot
into tiny crushed pieces?
Be flung in a dark wet corner
where no dog will bother to sniff you?
Thank you, dear eggshell, for being my friend
in this bleak hour,
for telling me that my present impotence
contains within itself a suggestion of power.
Or that's how I see it now.'

Ace got up from the table,
walked out into the street. There was nothing
in his heart for the moment but here was
a face to greet. It belonged to a child
playing a tin whistle
so badly, so out of tune
and with such remorseless dedication
Ace loved her immediately
as far as the other side of the moon
as deep as the river in his head.
He loved her with a love
as delicate as the eggshell
to which he had spoken.
He could not explain,
as he looked in the child's eyes,
why, though the city had more than
its share of broken men and women,
a small, frail, exquisite presence
remained unbroken.

A bit upsetting

In the radioactive light
        of British Nuclear Fuels
    apologists agree
it's a bit upsetting to see children of cancersperm
        crawl from the Irish sea
fathered–mothered by you and me.

    Making love
can be a deadly business
in the malignant light

    but Dr Albert Mundy
will answer all questions
after his lecture tonight.

Child

Sometimes, as I walk the streets
   of this snattering city
      I'm struck,
      listening to the voices
of some articulate bright men,
      by their instant
      willingness
to see the worst in everyone.

At such moments, I'm reminded
   I'm the child of a slave race
      and I mustn't complain
         if I see
      envy poxify a face.
On! On through the streets of sneer
      and the slavemind light.
I remind myself there are kind voices here.
      Maybe I'll hear one tonight.

Letter from China

'Though Dublin may be the arsehole of the world
   out here in China
      I miss it
and when I next descend to that gossiping stench
   I'll fall on my knees
      and kiss it.'

Letter to Ace: I want to tell the robins

'The robins are playing on the bridge today.

That mad March light gave me courage to face the fear
of seeing a fool reflected in the mirror.
    The air whispered to me –

                    "Yerra, fuck it,
which is better: being nothing at all
or a gadabout fool?"

The sun kissed my skin, I felt a smile
playing on my face.
            I was new.
            I believed in my own style.

I want to tell the robins
about your laughter, your words
opening these windows,
                        making me new,
            kissed by the sun
as I'd never been kissed by a man.

            You're gone
                and yet
                    you live in me,

    old man, old poet, old busy bee,
you gave me treasure that you'll never see.'

Not yet winter

The half-read letter
partners the half-read novel on the floor.
It's cold though not yet winter.
The alarm-clock winds itself into my brain.
Will I ever see you naked again?

Poem over

Ace read a poem to Kanooce one night
   when he felt so alone
he had to sing (or quote himself) to
   someone, anyone.
Poem over, Kanooce trotted out, returned
   ten minutes later to drop
   at Ace's feet
   a long bar of Toblerone.

On the school wall

She sits alone on the school wall
looking at the other girls
playing games she's never played
because she's daddy's special girl
and he gives her sweets and chocolate
and Seven-Up and Lucozade
and beats her when her mother
is out of the house
and has intercourse with her then.
Under her dress, she has welts on her body
and she knows she must never say a word
because he says he'll kill her if she does.
So she sits on the school wall
looking at the other girls playing games
listening to their laughter and happy screams
listening to their words
playing and frisking like robins in the hedges
enjoying their own lives,
private and free.

Shy child

'My father is an evil man,
   his only wish, to harm anyone
he can. I am
   the mother of my father's son.

I live deep in the country with a decent man.
I sit and watch the evening creep
like a shy child across the fields.
I fear my sleep.'

Legend

There are days in Dublin when the very notion-burden
of self is so unendurable
I belt out on my own
like some half-demented goblin
                from a legend claiming he
          is compelled to exist
       being dead when alive
  or alive when dead
in some gloomy fortress
            enshrouded in mist.

Down by the Liffey I meet them –
                 the legends
      singing Dublin exists in a way
neither the rich nor the poor can deny
      no matter how hard they try
        because the river
      is muttering as it bends
        and twists,
a story winding for fun among gathered friends,
      through the city and country,

'I am, am I not, yes I am, am I not, I I I
never lie, never lie, I'm a legend, a legend,
      that's why.'

He almost does but he does not

What is love, good quirkers, pray?
Ace whispers to the ship at
            the bottom of the sea.
The question is a spifflicated seabird
navigating heaven like a Video Nasty.

Not for the first time the seabird
                becomes a man
trying to be honest with his staggering heart
so packed with demons prompting him
to present his mediocrity as art
            he almost does
            he almost does

            but he does not

because one small bright suggestion
of love begins to grow
into a new man changing to a seabird
becoming the question flying through his mind
scanning heaven for an answer he'll never know.

I am Mary Crane

'The whole damned lot are out of the house.
God in heaven, it's great to be alone.
He was fine for a while but soon became
the most boring man I've ever known.
            These Sunday afternoons!
                Alone,
            most happily alone,
            all the kids gone too.
    Just lying here with nothing on
gives me this feeling of being true
to myself, somehow, as if for a short while
            I am Mary Crane

here in this room,
          Mary Crane
relaxing into my own
          style of being.
Let the world spin on its own axis,
     I lie here in the old privacy
and no man's eyes have ever diminished me.'

Midnight

Ace stood at midnight on O'Connell Bridge,
eyes on Anna squelching to the sea.
He closed his eyes, wondered, 'How many people
are fucking in Bluebell, Donnycarney,
Stoneybatter, the Vico Road and Pimlico just now?'
Anna said nothing, just wandered home.
Up there, the stars were unborn children
waiting their chances in the dark.
A drunk staggered past, cursing everyone
from Shrewsbury Road to the Phoenix Park,
cursing as if cursing were the ultimate privilege
witnessed by a solitary figure on O'Connell Bridge.

The nature of direction

That March night, I might have explored heaven
but instead I discovered hell.
Cadena answered, no sign of Helen.
Wrong bell.

Outside the ring

Doctor Moran is elegantly dressed today,
a future beckons, it must be promising,
she's going for interview. Why
does she remove her wedding-ring?

Hot bread

She smells my loneliness as if it were
    hot bread between her fingers.
'Let's go for a walk this evening,' she says.
    After twenty years her kindness lingers.

The old triangle

I love
    to believe
        in hope

Dramatis Personae

The mad father battles the sea.
The old bachelor wipes his arse with a
                        fist of grass.
Ace steps out of me
to test the streets of broken glass.

Blasting away

Ace is blasting away at his Europoem
poem to Homer Goethe Dante Camoëns Shakespeare
Blake, all the voices of obscure parishes
burdened with universality

His mind streels down a street in Portugal
pauses at a shrine in southern Spain
dips into a well-lit brothel in Berlin
suffers the dreary spits of Irish rain

Europoem is flaking right ahead
Ace is a map of that bashed old place
all the voices of the articulate dead
co-light to fight mind's darkness in his face

Blitzed-ignorant, three things he loves: gumption, gaiety, grace.

Rabbitarse

Ace broke the Maastricht Treaty
like a crust o' stale bread
then applied for an audience with the Pope
to discuss the foetus-dead.
His Holiness rejected the application.
Ace saw red.

  Red
 is what he saw.
  Yellow
 is what his guts are.
  White
 is what his skin is.

Did I say white? If you look closely
at Ace's skin, you'll see
it's a dirty brown.

There are times when Ace
has a face like a rabbit's arse
but this never stops the old bollocks
having noble thoughts
about, for example, the foetus-dead.

Noble Thoughts of Rabbitarse
is the title of his autobiography
in which he will disclose more
than he has ever dared to mention
    heretofore
about would-be creatures and would-be voices.

Rabbitarse Ace is determined to bring them in
from the cold of the universe
where they wander, says he, like flecks
trying to be raindrops or snowflakes.

Bring them in, says he. Let them be heard.

I hear. The stars are made of blood. My heart rejoices.

In the end was the word
and the word was a star made of blood.

Morning for Alice Gadden

She awoke, all pain. How many times had she been hit?
The black city was her morning spit.
There was blood in it.

Her father

'I walked with my father
   to Adam and Eve's
every Sunday morning
   through the city of Dublin

my father showed me
   God's grief and tears
I gave to heaven
   my small prayers

while outside the river
   flowed like the days
and inside the church
   the people sang praise

to the God beyond pain
   Whom we asked to come
like the light of dawn
   into our hearts
with his bread of love.'

Paul

Under a sky made of lead
when a man in not entirely mad
but holds on like a flea
between two thumb-nails

every moment is a revolution
threatening to break every bone in my head.

A pleasant afternoon.
Only the flies are lunatic.
Hold my hand, Loretto, your mother
has lumps in her breast.

Let's walk to the end of the street
and there part
carefully preserving whatever pictures we possess
of each other's heart.

I swear I'll not go mad
till the voices fascist my head.
Don't forget to write. Give
your love to Paul, he's funny,
clear-eyed and kind.

Imitations

I

I speak this morning (it recalls mornings
of frost and ice adding further danger
to that grim trudge through streets with no Warning
Signs to guide familiar local or lost stranger)

as a shithouse at the back of a National School
in a remote part of rural Ireland where
imitations of Laurel and Hardy acting the fool
for each other, for you and me, resonate in the air.

One by one, some shyly-tamely biding their time,
others with tears in their eyes, hands smarting
that they become the hope of this knotgrass nation,
children come to shit and piss in my friendly slime.
I've absorbed generations and am still carrying
the tears and fears of their grief-shot education.

II

Someone whitewashed me nine years ago.
I glowed as the children relieved themselves
in me. The year came for them to go
into a world waiting to make or break them

or simply leave them dull and unbroken,
capable of doing whatever they had to do.
I knew their dreams. If I'm not mistaken
I hear their names tonight, cold as drips of dew
on blades of grass: Eddie Morrissey,
Johnny Dee, Captain Dunne, the Buffer Hayes,
Jim Considine, Mike Tierney, Simon Grace.

Then it's England, Africa, America,
Australia, Canada, the Barbados,

stars whitewashed out of time and space.

Worried

'I'm worried about you, Brendan,' said the major poet,
'Yes, worried. Why are you so bitter?
I was reading your stuff last night and I
nearly wept at the note of true bitterness
you struck again and again. Is it because
the marriage went wrong? Is it the drink?
Long years of stupid boozing, self-deception?
Are you soured at what life has done to you?
Where did you go wrong? Why must
you sing such a bitter song?

Of course, I know a poet must be honest.
Honesty above all, that's what I say.
Honesty, even if it lands you in hell!

But it won't, of course. Beauty outlives the beast,
there's good all about us, imagine things that way,
show a little hope. You are, after all, alive and well.'

The major poet, friendly, concerned connoisseur of style
departed with an Irish fiver smile.

O'Connell Street encounter

I met Original Sin in O'Connell Street, Dublin,
looking very sad.
'What's wrong, Original?' I asked.
'Hard to say, hard to say,' Original replied
without a trace of vanity or pride,
'What I mean is, I can't find the words
for the way I think I feel I am.
This world is a pit of shame
where I live with a burning sense of being a fraud,
failing to live down to my name

which has a paradisal splendour when you think of it.
Original! Original Sin!
Maybe that radiant name went to my head
but now I feel robbed of my primalwit
and wisdom, I'm a joke, a cod, a fake, a nit, a hasbeen.
In short, a bit of a shit.
Everyone's committing me now, without a second thought.
I might as well be dead, I've lost
all my originality,' Original said.

Turns

'He stays away
three weeks six months a year
and then returns to say
(I can hardly believe my ears)

   "I love you I miss you I love you"

I look at him, bright, ruthless, tall,
lying to himself, and once again
I fall
and fall more deeply the bigger the lie.
He sits in the car lying, crying.
I sit with him. Am I still sane?
He goes to his wife. My turn to cry.
Why don't I tell him what I know he's doing?
Gone. Crawling. When will he come again?'

Ten years later

'A woman's worst mistake? Her self-sprung trap?
   The notion
            that she can change
                  a genuine bastard
                              into a genuine chap.'

Great lover

'You are,' she said 'a truly great lover,
passionate intentions, perfect moments, thrilling misses,
now a bull, now a ram, now a boy
running for cover from small kisses.'

Colleague

'She broke both legs, we soon forgot her.
If that woman was a horse we'd have shot her.'

Time being

Coming to the edge of hell
Ace saw the man the suit the smile
the house was clean and all was well
yet all would change in a little while

Cream

'My name,' she said 'is Amelia Vickers
and I want you to fuck me as soon as you can.'
'Why?' I asked, a perplexed, slightly excited man.
'Because whenever I see you, you cream my knickers.'

Distraction

Ace, distracted by the gypsy's naked breast
feeding her child in the August sun

did not complain when he discovered
every penny in his pockets gone.

Approaching Christmas

The child sucks sour milk from the bottle
while over his body
the black dress with small gold buttons and braid
lies lovingly.

His mother, beautiful and stinking
of sweat, piss and grease,
sinks in the old armchair
reading *War and Peace*.

Wave

The wave libertied up from the Liffey.
Ace escaped the murderous water
and thought, 'I'd rather be assassinated for
                      my barbing
than honoured for my caution.'

Demons

'The maddest fuckin' head in Dublin, demons
         tryin' to break the cage.'
         He smiled.
'But ya love the demons, don't ya?
Where wud ya be widdout yar rage?'

Wrinkles

Now and then, Ace's face grew foreign to him.
He considered his wrinkles, recoiled, plunged into
Beauty and Health Consultant, Augustine Mc Grill
who advised him to try Natures' newest breakthrough
in battling wrinkled skin, Natural Thrill,
not a cream, lotion or gel
but made from safe ingredients
including fish protein extract, marine plants,
zinc, calcium and vitamin C.
Its first clinical trial in a Dublin hospital
(one of the few not closed down
in that coughing, muttering town
given to verse celebrating its status
as the centre of the paralysis of the universe)
showed a substantial improvement, after three months,
in wrinkling, mottling and dryness

among fifty women aged forty to sixty-nine
and a half, with average skin thickness improving
by eighty-two per cent
and elasticity by twenty-five.
More alive! More alive! More alive!
Ace tried it, it was like
having a face-lift without the surgery
and it made him feel good inside
till one day he looked in the mirror
and heard himself say,
'God in heaven, but I miss my wrinkles!
I miss my wrinkles!' Then and there,
he ended his affair with Natural Thrill
and let his wrinkles have their way,
rioting through and over his skin
like little saucyjack old men
with jokes of their own
and pains of their own
and a primy, pushy, shrivelling life
utterly their own.
They were like worn books
yesterday's ideas
repeated old stories of randy nights
            – his wrinkles had a right
               to this life of their own.
Suddenly, exquisitely alone
Ace bowed his head
and apologised to his wrinkles
vowing never again
to interfere.
He washed, towelled his face,
took to the streets
letting his wrinkles live again
            like himself,
            a late
            twentieth century
            puzzled, going somewhere-nowhere,
            uglyish man
            who enjoyed his wrinkles
            as he enjoyed his farts

dreaming of money
            women
damp delights of nowhere-home
            and now and then
the perfect weather of foreign parts.

Winner

'He'll never punch like the Mannassa Mauler
  but he'll win through
'cos he's a great little crawler.'

Paunch

When Ace fondled his paunch
questions invaded his mind:
'What foodmountains went to produce
this shapeless wambling rumbling blind
memorial stretching out like the future
in front of me? Where
are the endless gins and whiskeys,
garrulous nights of swilling beer,
the sips, swigs, gulps, sweeties, crunchies,
nuts, chockies, fruitos, midnight feasts?
Where is the talk that knew no fear,
the lightning solutions to cosmic problems?
Where is the skill that frightened the beasts?
And where are the fucks of yesteryear?'

Nail

Drunk, he staggers through the streets
  of the hopelessly sober town.
The nail that sticks out is the first
  to be hammered down.

Everything Molly said

Molly the waitress asked me, 'What's up
with your man, Ace de Horner?
He thinks he's a genius, he thinks he's
doin' you a favour when he says good mornin',

he thinks his shit is ice-cream.
O pardon me, sir, that just popped out,
don't worry, it'll pop back in.
But why does Ace de Horner walk about
with a dog as ugly as Original Sin?

Kanooce is the dog's name, sir. Funny name. Kanooce.
But Jesus, sir, that dog would ate
a farmer's arse though a hedge.

Kanooce's jaws are always drippin' juice
like blood, or blood like juice. Sooner or later,
he'll gobble a tinker on O'Connell Bridge
or some poor soul in Westmoreland Street.
And what will Ace de Horner do about that?'
'I don't know,' I replied, 'I just don't know'.

Molly was worried. Then she said
'Mr de Horner is always talkin' about the poetic art
but the world would be a safer place
if poets and killerdogs were kept apart.
Would you tell that to the Taoiseach, sir,
or write a letter to the paper?'

'I'll convey your message to the Arts Council,'
I replied, 'I'll tell them all you've said,
down to the last word.'

I did. I received, after two months, a note
pulsating with gratitude, ending with
'We'll take everything that Molly said on board.'

Something about the gods of prose

Kanooce sank his fangs into the novelist's left buttock
at the junction of Lemon Lane and Grafton Street.
Bewley's venerable coffee-house resounded
with the novelist's howls of pain. He put
his hand back and found
two holes in his arse,
one from God, the other from Kanooce.
His howls got worse
and he bolted among a rather
gorgeous arrangement of imported flowers,
scattering them in the frosty weather
like neat sentences suddenly gone berserk
after all that work
without which no lasting art can happen
to touch this and future generations.
Kanooce, too, bloodromped among the flowers,
bits of the novelist's buttock
dripping like bad grammar from his jaws
and, alarming to report, eager for more.
What on earth will satisfy that pitbull whore?
Kanooce didn't care what laws he broke,
he was simply buttock-mad at the moment.
The poor novelist, determined
to hang on to the remainder
of what God had given him,
hopped, bleeding, into a taxi
and sped away, safe to haven
and hospital.
                    (The taxi-driver, a dry
alcoholic, odd bod, seemed moved by,
and detached from, this bleeding frolic
as he negotiated the pitiless traffic
with eyes both sad and laughing
seeing how sane blends coyly with horrific.
Well, why shouldn't it, for Art's sake? The thought
was sharp enough to raise
unchronicled orgies of his drinking days.
Forget. One must forget. All
that matters now is that I get
this bleeding arse to hospital.)

Kanooce stood in the street and chewed the buttock
like a gravid reader of post-modern prose.
In the taxi, the deconstructed novelist
breathed seven Book of the Dead sighs of relief.
In Grafton Street, Kanooce scanned the sea of buttocks
hoping to find
another suitable protuberance
he might bring to grief.
Grief would welcome it
because grief accommodates all comers.
In Ireland's most prosperous street
there were so many things
an idle dog might do,
so much well-nourished human meat
for him to chew
like thought, like tufts of thought.

Alone,
at the corner of Lemon Lane,
Kanooce stands looking out for novelists again.
Something about the gods of prose
turns him on.

Restoration drama

After several operations, the novelist's left buttock was restored.
He grew wiser, older,
talked less, wrote more, went for long solitary walks,
glancing regularly over his shoulder.
Back home, at his desk, his blood was hotter, vision colder.

Rules

A winter fire: rising from his study
of the strict rules of Gaelic prosody
            in the bardic period
and in eighteenth-century folk poetry

Ace de Horner quit his Bluebell pad
and strolled with Kanooce
along the stinking Liffey that yet
was crammed with lovejuice, lifejuice,

until they came to O'Connell Street
where a bagwoman was being mugged.
They walked on.
The rules danced demandingly in Ace's head.
Kanooce ate a poodle. Ace bought fresh carrots.
They turned for home.

The rules were waiting there.
Ace got Offaly turf to rouse the dying fire.
The flameshapes stirred, grew, leaped, spread like
                        pain or laughter.
Kanooce growled with unruly feeling
at shadows acting assassins between floor and ceiling.
What rules will bring the killing shadows to heel?

That way

On a pensive summer day
Ace saw Catullus
walk that way,
pissed out of his tree,
returning from the Galway
Races where he'd won a ton,
backing a horse called
Hareypass Hibernicus
at thirty-three
to one.

Coming back to Dublin
Catullus stopped
at Kinnegad
and began to drink
at a daft rate
whiskey and Guinness
till he felt bad.
Between Kinnegad and Dublin
Catullus stopped
at various hostelries
and crammed his guts with the hard stuff.
His triumphant journey
became a reeky odyssey,
a stumbling mumbling frushing blunder.
He cursed the barmen
in every town
so 'twas no wonder
he got the bum's rush
out of every pub he stank in.
As well, his cash began to dwindle
and in the end
he groped in vain
for pound mark yen franc dollar.
Nothing.
That's when Ace saw Catullus
walk that way
and heard him say
'I wish to Christ
I was a sober bloody scholar!'

The moaning sea

Nobody knows that ultimate bad dream
which makes Kanooce tremble and diminish
but there's another dream he dreams
that, when he barks it, never fails to astonish

Ace de Horner, who keeps copious notes
on all dreams he has and hears about.

172

Kanooce dreams this:
                        on a rock he squats
in the middle of the Irish Sea, waves at
his paws and nose. Slowly, before his eyes
forty thousand aborted foetuses float past
followed by young women out of Ireland drowning
in their own cries.
                        A demon screams at Kanooce,
'Eat them! Eat them!' but our hero freezes,
refuses, stares at the moaning
sea of people born, unborn, living, dead.

He wakes up then, and crawls into Ace's bed.

                Kanooce is deepawake.
                    The dream continues.
                        Kanooce whimpers.
The demon said what the demon said.

Out of the visioncloud

I'm fed-up looking at you, Kanooce, said Ace,
I want you to look at me,
I want you to tell me what you see.
A visioncloud passed over Kanooce's face
and a voice barked out of its heart –
            How do I know
            what Satan thinks of Milton
            or Poldy Bloom
            of Mr Joyce
            or Crazy Jane
            of Mr Yeats
            or Heaven and Hell
            of Mr Blake
            or Cuchulain
            of Anonymous?
            All this poetry
            is so one-sided
            so one-minded
            it's truly insane
            perhaps insanely true.

Therefore, Mr Ace de Horner
let me sing
in barking verse
precisely what I think of you!

No! No! No! screamed Ace, not now, not here,
I want to see it as I see it, not
as you think I ought to, and certainly
not as you do.
The way I see it is the way that's true
for me
and therefore
everyone I see.
So no more barking in that insolent fashion!

Kanooce looked at his master.
The visioncloud passed away.
How Ace sees it is the way to see it.
Three people go blind in Ireland every day.
What else can a faithful pitbullterrier say?

Over Kanooce's face shades that rare, strange smile.
Ace opens his eyes and drowns in his own style.

That garment

Ace de Horner bought his IRA trenchcoat
at an auction in Arbour Hill prison.
What changes swept through his soul
the moment he slipped it on!
He knew the thrill of murdering
a young man home on Christmas leave,
he knew the pleasure of bombing
anyone anywhere anytime,
phones rang in his blood
as he issued warnings of disaster,
he enjoyed the intellectual certainty
of knowing who is the victim, who the master,

he knew history as it should be known
and must be re-shaped,
he was a hungerstriking poet, an object
of police brutality, a freedom fighter,
lover of justice, seeker of peace
moulding a future for decent workers.

When Ace wore his trenchcoat
he led revolutions all over the globe,
translated fiery songs of rebellion
and planted seeds of hope.

When he came home
he left his dripping trenchcoat in the hall,
prepared a hot whiskey with cloves
and brooded on the meaning of it all.
The trenchcoat dripped
lyrical drops of Wicklow rain
like shy, charming drops of blood.
After a long walk, hot whiskey, piss of solitude,
Ace was feeling good.
Kanooce had the flu and stretched in peace
beside a healing fire.
Ace took pen and recycled paper
and started to write.
Shuddering changes began to rip the world,
the seas were seas of light,
rivers were veins of perception, mountains
monuments of insight.
Firelit Ace was in his glory now,
his trenchcoat slowly dripping,
the cosy flames were immortal dancers
and Kanooce was snoring.

Sniff

Kanooce is always sniffing Ace's psyche
   layered with agony and nightmare.
When Kanooce sniffs it, sniffs it, Ace cries 'Crikey!
What the hell d'you think you're doin' there?
Why can't you leave my poor psyche rest
   among its riddles and contradictions,
     sick ironies and visionary zest
unknown to bankers, academics, politicians,
in short, the necessary horror of my days?
         No more sniffing,
         dear Kanooce,
         no more sniffing,
let my psyche loiterfester in horrific peace.'

   But devil the rest will Kanooce give Ace
until, sniffed to Bedlam, de Horner begins to sing
like the happymad poets of hectic Greece.

        If
        Ace sings like this,
        why should Kanooce not
        sniff?

Career

Ace is bent on a notable poetic career
but now and then the fears mount
in his heart. What, he asks himself, if these
critical buggers don't take me into account?

What if they insist I'm a stuffed eccentric
living alone with a pitbullterrier?
Suppose they decide I've a lousy technique,
am no poet at all, but a versifying gurrier?

What if they say I'm nothing without Kanooce,
my loyal pal, the sniffer-sharer of my dream?
Ace tried to calm himself:

176

'What is this fear?
What is the meaning of blame and praise?
And what in hell is a poetic career?'

Kanooce approached. He knew Ace needed a lick.
His tongue roughed Ace in the right place. That did the trick.

Trouble

Ace gets drunk at times. His eyes are flames,
his mind is fire, his tongue a wild rover.
He sobers up. The trouble with Ace?
When he's not drunk he's sober.

Eating a star

Ace and Kanooce strolled across O'Connell Bridge
Liffey chucklingsobbing underneath
like a secret history of women,
enough to take your breath

away if you studied it
but what dog or poet has time for that?
Kanooce and Ace were passing Eason's Bookshop
when Kanooce stopped, stared at

Madonna, star of sex, on the cover
of a not inexpensive book in the window.
Kanooce leaped, sank his fangs in the goddess,

tore her to pieces, began licking her
pieces with a vigour to induce vertigo
in onlookers. (There were many). Poor, dizzy, pop-eyed Ace!

Poor poet! Poor dog! Poor star of sex!
Poor star of all the seas!

Liffey slides on, slimey with secret histories.

Daring the dream

Now and then, Ace de Horner dared the dream
that lifted him out of the selfpit,
stripped him for homage to the girl
playing the fiddle at the corner of Grafton Street.

For once, he stopped looking at himself
and looked at her. Her. She filled his mind,
he walked through street after street, crossing the gulf
in his heart and began to know how blind

he was. For a moment he thought he'd be terrified
but his seeing his blindness filled him with joy
and made him see people for the first time,

that time before he stretched and grew afraid
of the words and eyes of the feral boy
laughing at the prisoner he would become.

Mild

Why this compulsion in Ace
    to sit and imagine evil
        till it flows from his eyes
            like blood from the body
of a man or a woman
    or a child
        bombed to pieces
            by people
                whose spokesman
                    on the radio
                        next day

is so mild,
    so terrifyingly
        mild?

178

Obsession

Ace spent years writing a poem
obsessing him since childhood,
now a stretch of peace, now a storm
aching to be born of his blood,

pleading for its own life, free of his.
He laboured to release the prisoner
seeking, year in year out, right words for those
elusive moods and pictures demanding their

freedom, their right to be whatever they were.
The day he thought he'd finished the poem
he went for a walk, alone, leaving it on the floor

page upon page upon page. When he returned, there
sat Kanooce, jaws chomping, chomping.
He'd eaten Ace's poem for dinner.

Ace wept, wept, heart stabbed by the old thorn.
A devoured obsession is an obsession re-born.

Will I listen?

I know a man with something to say.
  Will I listen?

  A sudden April wind
      flicks several petals
  from a cherrytree I love
      and blows them away.

Brief gift

Convinced he was a drab criminal of hell
   Ace arrested himself one night
         stuck himself in jail
in a dirty narrow smelly cell
   from which, nonetheless, he could see
stars of such bewitching variety,

              when he tried and judged
              himself next morning

he let himself go free.

No freedom Ace had ever known
compared with this brief gift to himself.
He wished he could offer it to others
but he knew it'd be exhausted
before nightfall.

But Janey Mary it was great while it lasted!

North Korean light

Who is the man calling
Ace in the middle of the night
warning

him that the American
Monetary System
is about to collapse

with smithereening effects on life
in Bluebell and other
places in and out of hell.

The warning comes in a soft
voice, so firmly soft Ace knows
it is not daft

but true to its own
North Korean light,
where it's calling from.

Ace takes the warning to heart,
quits the Bluebell cell
at three in the morning

and wanders through Dublin
Kanooce at his side.
Nobody acknowledges him.

He's like an old dinosaur-poet
who might benefit from listening
to stories of the magic carpet.

He trudges the streets
of monetary collapse,
much the same as they looked

yesterday afternoon.
What will happen?
More crime? Famine come again?

Skeletons everywhere?
Scrawny Kanooce chewing bones at will?
Shall we call it war

or just an endless, brutal, accepted
sense of people screwing
each other every way they can?

Dawnlight is weak and scary
for the troubled walker.
Past the silent temple of Janey Mary

he downheads, lovelight struggling
to shine through.
What will happen to his darling?

How will she live?
Will she witness the final proof
of the piteous waste of his love?

A ludricous moon, like a drunken self, grins at him
as he returns to the Bluebell cell:
home

still standing. Kanooce laps
the day's first dollop of milk.
Ace sips a blessed cup of coffee.

All day he'll brood on money
(myth? material?) and be as ignorant at night
as he is at morning

though he knows it's a sound
like breathing, like people's blood
through their veins carolling

or the sea touching
the shores of the world
purging, receding, eroding, warning.

Considering

Three broken windows
    in a derelict house
        on the edge of the Liffey.

A crow flies in from slumwhere
    squats in the middle window,
        considers the river.

Ace leans on his walking stick,
        considers his brother.

In the blink of an eye the crow
        considers the poet and shows him
            how to fly.

Digging

Ace sniffed and probed the centuries like laneways,
tasting the bits and bobs of the pre-Irish dig.
No man has lived, he thought, who has not prayed
in the cunt of Sheila na Gig.

A line

Moran denied him, treating him
                    like the dumbest of men.
Ace wrote a line.
                    Moran never denied him again.

Wet grass

You succulent bitch, he murmured,
I'll eat you yet.
I love your cannibal style, she said,
but the grass is wet.

A new fool

Some driver hit and killed
that blackandwhite dog last night.
This morning, all the cars
stress the creature's flattened carcase.

Whoosh! Whoosh! Wheels fly over
the blackandwhite thing in the middle
of the road. Ten yards away, Ace de Horner
stands and peers at the flashing faces

of the drivers. From time to time he glances
at blackandwhite. It could be me, he thinks,
it could be me, and what difference would it be?
These drivers have somewhere to go and not God

in all his upthere will come between them and their
whatever-it-is. Where's the dog's head? Legs? Tail?
Never interfere with a man driving somewhere.
Stand there, peering, peering, one more helpless fool.

Ace is a new fool, there are times he feels compassion
ridiculously, as now, for the whooshed blackandwhite,
for the drivers too, for himself looking on,
for the whole damned city, frantic lump of shite.

Without flaw

The obscenest thing I ever heard
was a most sophisticated word
uttered without flaw
by a gentleman of the law
at a dinner-party where
the cream of the land
was rich and rare.
What was I doing there?
Same as here.

She sang of peace

I met Christ the woman in Dublin today.
Her face was lined, her hair grey.
She held the world upside-down in her right hand
and she sang of peace in Ireland.

Isle of Manpower

'Does it work?' I ask. The air is ice.
'Well, I never whipped the same arse twice.'

Pact

No trouble. They sign. No nervous cough.
Peace is a moment when murder pays off.

Christ and the little key

Out there, bestial hearts know love.
In here, we kill it but plough on, plough on,
unearthing lies of definition and solution
to this fear of simply not letting it happen

which is, Ace believes, what he wishes to achieve:
witness the mess, listen for music,
have some word for the begging children
see eyes condescending or accusing or blind,
let them knife through you,
carry the bags, climb the steps, open the door
thanking Christ and the little key
you have been here before.

Odd thing

The odd thing about this poet-assassin
is that when he himself starts versing
he drools nostalgia. Where is the man's
genius for cursing?

Or what in hell's name has he been rehearsing?

Bewley's coarse brown bread (unsliced)

There are days when Ace
can't begin to be human
till he feeds the seagulls

worrying the Liffey. He buys
a loaf of Bewley's coarse brown bread
(unsliced), plods through the eyes

of Westmoreland Street, turns left
at O'Connell Bridge, heads for
the wall, breaks the bread,

starts to feed the shrieking
creatures of whatever heaven
hangs over scuttery Dublin

like a letter begun by a fallen
angel with a nice writing style
millions of years ago, still

being written by hordes of
angels and demons, manky chancers,
chatty conmen, parodists of love

and hate, parodists of parody itself. Alone
at the wall, he watches the ravenous
birds come into their own,

breaking the bread from the generous
waters of old mother Liffey
(how she flows for you for me for all of us!)

and slowly, like light stealing
through the overcoat dark of a winter morning
a feeling, a small real feeling

of being human invades old Ace (hard
enough to come by these days). He feeds the birds
till the sign of a smile crosses his face.

Not for the first time he thanks
the insatiable gulls. Soon he'll walk
past restaurants shops churches banks

more human with every step.
(Would the gulls eat him, properly prepared?)
Who knows their ferocious snow? He may let it rip

tonight, find something new in this parodyplace,
this black pool of cynical skins
and quite unoriginal sins,

some new slant on the gathering dark,
gossip lighting up living and dead,
the fabulous power of coarse brown bread

bobbing on the river
slowly creating the sign of a smile
auguring a hurt unkillable style.

The soul's loneliness

it's nothing to go on about
but when I hear it
in the ticking of the clock

beside the books and photographs
or see it in the shine
of an Eason's plastic bag at midnight

or touch it in the tree I call
Christ there outside my window
swaying in the day's afterglow

I shiver a little at the strangeness
of my flesh, the swell of sweat,
the child's poem I'll never forget

and find my eyes searching the floor
for a definition of grace
or a trace of yourself I've never noticed before.

Cross of screams

The Mouth spittles down on Ace in Westmoreland Street
and begins to chew him:
chew chew chew – his ears and eyes vanishing,
his tongue, brain, each attentive limb,

and still The Mouth chews

not with teeth but with gossip and scandal,
yarns of money, drugs, violence, sex, lewd
accounts of bonds and buggery from Dublin to Donegal.

Then The Mouth zooms in on Ace himself,
proving how venal are his mind and art,
vile rhythms, shite-steeped lines, mean dreams.

Ace is eaten to nothing, is he? Gathering what's left
of bone and sinew, he hauls himself away
from The Mouth, dragging a cross of screams.

Behind him, in Westmoreland Street, The Mouth
stares at people, strides for a train, heads North.

Gospel country. The third bombing. The chewed earth.

Rain is the audience now

The Mouth is rapping on about having
it off in the bad old days in London
before most of his audience had started shaving
or grown to know the newold wickedness of Dublin.

The brothels pour from The Mouth as do whores
and dens in Soho and other places:
'Wisha, Christ in heaven, boys, I forget more
about life than ye'll ever know.' Young faces

agree, seem to agree. The Mouth raps on.
It's France now, Paris, Rouen, Marseilles.
Japan next, the shagging miracles of Tokyo.

The youngsters begin to drift away. The Mouth
stands there, bulging with himself. Rain
is the audience now for our can-o'-maggots Romeo

who's had every Molly Malone in the streets of Alive-Alive-O.

After prophecy

The Mouth is prophesying Civil War
conjuring an island of blood
              for every available ear.
                          Listen! Listen!

'The Protestants will murder the Catholics.
Terrorists will rule the land.
All your families will be endangered.
Peace will never be found.'

After prophecy, The Mouth climbs a hill by the sea,
     squats near a bed of flowers,
mumbling, rifling his brains for further horror

because it is his solemn duty
to tell the unenlightened millions
why they must live through an age of terror.

The Mouth never asks himself why he talks like this.
Should he put that question, would he wonder
if the horror of war is preferable to the horror of peace?

Lovers all

The Wexford Opera Festival; a very yes hotel;
table with guests; The Mouth in global swing
telling how he played hell
with a politician's reputation.
                         Guests are listening
in giggling enchantment.
                     'First, I spread the yarn
that Hopkins was a secret alco screwing
a businessman's wife from Dublin 4. Then
I added this poxy whore from Stoneybatter
plus a brothel in Fairview. Next, the drugs
spiced with a deal, half a million, what a ball!'

The Mouth looks good in evening dress, fitter
than he's been for seasons. His audience
grins. Thanks for the nuggets. Time for the Opera. Lovers all.

A modest proposal

The Mouth tried modest words on Janey Mary
ending with come to bed.
She fettled him a light seraphic smile.
Piss off, a ghrá, she said.

One thing, one thing only

She read the morning paper
listened to radio that day
looked at television that night
heard friends, sons and daughters
talk till after midnight.

One thing, one thing only.

She sat in the pitchdark on the edge of her bed.

'They need another famine,' she said.

If me granny could see me now (maybe she does)

'Smell me,' Janey Mary said.
Ace nosed her all over: 'You bring heaven into bed.'
'I'm from Dublin, lover.'

'So what if the National Debt increases?'

'So what if the North Koreans blow us all to pieces?'

'So what if me granny could see me now?
          O Jesus, maybe she does.'

'So what if the roads become one big grave?'

'So what if there's nobody left to save?'

'Enough sowhattery! Smell me!' she said.
He did, till his head was her head, her head his head.
Two heads become one.
Imagine!

By such unities are men undone
and women driven whacky in the noonday sun.

Old Irish love-song

For too long now,
Patrick Imelda Xavier Hayes,
you have been loitering
with intent.
Please take your tongue
out of my cunt.
There must be better ways
to pay
the rent.

Encouragement

'There's a bee in your milk, Janey Mary.'
'Travel on. You may find the honey.'

Definition

If Ace could define
what's eating him
he might encounter any man

or woman in the town
and not fear him or her.
Aching for definition

he lives in pained bewilderment,
the kind that guarantees
days and nights of casual torment,

a ravenous curiosity
concerning the sense of being
eaten alive, slowly.

He thinks of Imelda Coe
who told him in some detail
of a week of gluttony

in Paris: 'Why, it turned me
into a perfect lady
with a shrewd knowledge of the body

politic, private, religious, sexual.
I gorged myself into an awareness
of the meaning of hell,

a sound basis for the kind
of education necessary
to survive on this island.'

He remembers Eleanor Flood:
'I go days without hearing a voice,
no-hearing makes me feel good

until I want to taste a brain,
chew the words of someone
commenting on sun or rain.'

Everyone is eating everyone else,
thinks Ace, as he feels
his own reliable old pulse

beating softly in his darkness
linking him to gods who know
how to curse or bless

a creature being eaten alive
by himself or another.
What is it? A refusal to live?

A gradual drowning in bitterness?
A love of what is known as failure?
A loathing of what is called success?

A ferocious indignation at what himself
and others are doing to language
although they swear they're not?

How long does it take
for someone to be eaten to nothing?

Hey! It's time for a joke

so listen carefully.
   Can you hear me?
      What do you think of me,

me, the daddy of laughter
and elaborate ridicule
causing, as always, an appropriate stir?

Sorry for intruding, Ace.
I simply had to tell you a good one
when I saw the state of your face

in Westmoreland Street today.
I just wanted to relieve you a little
knowing the torment never goes away

but lives, real as stone,
yet, like a sky the colour of stone,
is beyond definition

as far as I can see. How far is that?
Can't say. I may consult a philosopher
or a Liffey rat

or both. Plato up to his neck
in mud, rat nibbling his lips, is
the man for me. He'll do the trick.

A drop from Ace's Nutbook

I think therefore I am
not sure of what I think
That may be why I just don't give a damn
and have a tendency to drink.

Birds of morning

pigeon fluffs the space between Ace and the sun
magpie slices the sky into good or bad
      luck for someone
bluetit chirps on the window-sill for bread
crows of nightmare go on croaking
      in his head

Clarification

The scarred man silenced Ace with 'I'm one of these
    who bombed their way to peace.
Let me clarify that a little more:
I'm a midnight knock on your door.'

A future with nobody

Ace met nobody at the Abbey Theatre.
They shook hands.
For as long as the future lasted
they were friends.

There goes nobody

there goes nobody
down by the river
nobody in search of something
nobody looking for somebody
nobody trying to be somebody
       at the same time

nobody drinks the city
eats the streets with no-eyes
listens to love and hate with no-ears
smells death and pride with no-nose

nobody knows more than nobody

if you let nobody into your heart
you'll cease to be afraid of nothing
like people who are somebody

where is nobody going?

to the usual place
by the river
into yesterday
by the long laneways
into the heartland of the unborn
by the endless roads of perplexity
nobody has grown to love

love?

that's what the pen said
that's what the computer will say
in spite of hardware and software
in the seagull light of dawn

       nobody
       nobody

the neatest nobody you never saw
the daringest nobody that never broke the law
avatar nobody embodying starglory
ructions nobody hissing poems of revolution
writer nobody in the mindpit of no-self
    tempted to think he's somebody

196

there goes nobody
learning to play the drum
doing a thesis on the angels
discoursing on rain
mentioning Spring
pleased and dazzled by the whole recurring thing

        nobody

to whom nothing happens
never had a thought
never asked why
was never bullied by punctuation
or dreams of his dead father
or pains in his ribs
or messy failure with somebody
   who is somebody else
the strangest creature in creation
           go softly
           so softly

don't wake nobody
sleep is well learned
let nobody sleep
let nobody wake
let nobody stroll by the river
whispering
of terrible untellable things
while the blackbird of Bluebell
      turns in his sleep
          a seagull threatens
              a crow grows more crowy
   a wagtail sips immortal water
    a lark revises a Mozart melody
      and nobody
          (there goes nobody)
           sings

Dirty penny

'If you do that again,' she spat,
'I'll charge you with sexual harassment.'
He took a dirty penny from his pocket,
            showed it to her, up close.
She smiled because she knew what that meant.

The stroller's view

The ageing liar lay
on Sandymount Strand,
his transcendental signifier
in Janey Mary's hand.
A young man, nearby, strolling into eternity,
seemed to understand.

Thoughts

'Thought is a flea in your pit, Janey Mary.'
'Thought is what tickles your prick, darling Ace.'
'Will you share a thought with me, my dearie?'
'What do you think when I lie in your face?'

Cockling through woods

Ace is a twitch, a complaint, a snore, scruffy
Orpheus off through the woods on his own.
    What is the old cockle looking for
in woods from which most of the birds are gone?

Imagine the twit in the light of dawn.

Walk

Ace took an image for a walk
past the old Mill where the soldiers
died fighting for something forgotten,
past the massive housing estate
where people kinda lived,
past the oldest university in the country,
sleeping,
past the creeping colours of autumn
in that handsome street where he'd been
beaten up (deservedly) in the old nights.
The image was fascinated, somewhat non-plussed.
When they got home the image said
'Thank you for showing me these strange places,
I shall go to my own place now,
set in a spot of acid starlight,
and dream of what I have seen. I'll return later
and slip into your head. It may be
I'll change you in ways you don't expect.
Or maybe you'll change me!'

Ace smiled goodbye. 'I'll see,' he said, 'I'll see.'

To where, again,

Sometimes, Ace is a question without an answer,
sometimes, an answer without a question.
No point asking which is which
or how he came to understand
what he didn't even realise he'd said
in reply to words knifing him like ice,
leaving him dispirited and free.
So, quitting a roomful of articulate faces,
he turns again to the river
knowing he is walking a street
where a man was kicked to death
the night before. Questions are being asked,
questions leading to the man who booted
another man out of this life into
...What? Who knows? Who can begin to know?
If that litterbin could talk...or that bus-stop...
Things that know the story keep their traps shut.
Ace hugs the river, the lipping dancing lights.
Why does he see the river as the dancer
leading him away from talk and murder
to where, again, he is an answer without a question
and again, a question without an answer?

A timely offer

One day, Ace saw time running out.
It was puffy, red in the face, limping on and on.
Ace asked time if it needed a helping hand.
No, it replied, I'll manage. But thanks for the offer, man.

A different madness

Ace sees the young man in Grafton Street
    saying his poem to the Easter crowd
in a voice now strident, now sweet,
    lifting his hands dancing hands to his head
as he tells of the beast in his sleep
    driving him on through seven kingdoms,
from which he returns, his dander up,
    his eyes changed to a pair of glow-worms

challenging the night and everything in it
    like the young man himself facing the crowd
looking, half-interested, at this shameless madness

    singing beyond itself.

                    Ace cannot do that,
not anymore, his is a different madness now,
a slow, cold pain he must celebrate and bless
            even as his heart must greet
                    the old defeat.

He is water now

he stands on O'Connell Bridge
    looking down the Liffey
of wheeling and crying birds

and they are all crying inside him
    and he is water now
water and cries and silence
beggars and money and cold night air

    and his shivering mind
        is thinking there
            without any words,
shivering, thinking there
        without any words

The man in black

looks at me askance
when I suggest
he may be organising Christ
out of existence

Choices

live
    veil
        vile
           evil

Hello

he'd never spoken to her
except to say hello
wherever he met her
in Bluebell or Pimlico

and she said hello back
always, always gentle
and quiet, hello, once,
and they both passed on

their ways in all kinds
of weather, neither knew
where the other was going,
they just moved without

touching or stopping, never
stopping or touching.
One day he said hello
and she said nothing.

Surprised, he stopped and
said hello again but
she said nothing, just
turned her head, walked

away. He often saw her after
that and always said hello
but never again did she
reply, never did she reply

and he never asked why,
he never dared ask why.

The leaf of love

Love is a leaf in Dawson Street in October
        and where did it come from?
    She was there, she was there,
    he was convinced he could remember
        but when he rang a voice said
'This is a Telecom Éireann Service announcement:
    the number you have dialled
        is an unconnected number.
                Thank you.'

He bent, lifted the leaf, turned it over, over in his hand.
A veined, varied miracle. He was glad he wasn't blind.
By the leaf of love is a slubbery man defined.

Who knows her touch?

Janey Mary hops off her bicycle
runs back the road
picks up three leaves.

Who knows what she feels?
Who knows her touch
when she bends and heals

though a scumbag mocks her
a gurrier slags her gewter
and a vandal smashes both wheels?

Who hobble and limp

Ace hobbles down the riverways
knows the heart of the limping dog
blood of the begging girl
dragging her feet behind her
in chilly October air.
Why does he haul himself around
like an injured man
being dragged from an accident?
Why does he dream of moving
as once he moved through the streets
of crush and babble and getting there?

He senses the body and mind of winter.

They were said to be blessed:
the lost, the lonely, the hungry, the peacemakers.

And a thought perches on his heart:

blessed are those who hobble and limp
for they shall run
like the deer above in the Phoenix Park.

God's mercy

Robert Emmett, eloquently dead,
looks over everybody's head
and never looks down.

Janey Mary stands at the gate
of Saint Stephen's Green
where the most rhythmical buttocks in this
    part of the earth may be seen
and says, looking at The Gents among the trees,

            'Isn't it God's mercy
            that the men of Dublin
            can go for a piss
            in the woods in the middle of
                    this dirty old town!'

Dirty word

When Ace heard it he wanted
to touch it with his heart.
It was a dirty word, so dirty
he decided to take it home
and clean it.
So back to the Bluebell pad
with him, the dirty word
in his pocket wrapped in
a nice clean hankie.
He boiled a pot of water
and dropped the word in it
for a bubbling hour.
Then he took it out
and scrubbed it with gusto
for another hour or so.
The word was getting less
dirty but by no stretch
of the tongue or imagination
could it be called spotless.

Ace disinfected it
with three full containers
of Johnson's Fresh Duck Disinfectant
guaranteed to kill germs
and leave toilets
hygienically clean.
Back in the boiling water
again, take it out, apply
two plastic bottles
of Harpic Limescale Remover
guaranteed to dissolve all
carbonate limescale deposits
where germs can breed
and stains take hold.
More boiling water, more
scrubbing. Then Kanooce gave it
a severe licking.
This did the trick.
The dirty word was clean
or cleaner than it had been
since it was born. When
did that word begin
its life in the mouths of men
who'd made it so vile
it had lost all sense
of its own original style?
Now, as Ace looked at it
attentively, lovingly,
he could see a good deal
of its primal beauty
and his renewed eyes made
him feel the need to apologise
to the word.
'I'm sorry,' he whispered, 'I'm sorry.'
It was a simple word
yet magical, magical.
Ace found himself
saying it over and over
and over and over
until the magic stole
into his heart for a moment
and he felt like
a burst of birdsong.
Honest to God, he did!
Ace de Horner, a burst of birdsong!

He felt so birdsongy, in fact,
he opened the door of his pad
and let the word out
into the streets once more,
wishing it the best of luck
from his briefly magical heart
as it tasted the Bluebell air
and flew away
to take its chances again
in the minds and the mouths of men.

Clean language

Ace finds it hard to understand
why Grapevine Smiley's language is so clean
because Grapevine has been licking arses
since the challenge began
and there's never a dirty word in what he writes.
Grapevine is a good man.

Buzzword

Did he snap it up from a paper
one Sunday morning sitting in Stephen's Green
    absorbing the story
of a Princess becoming a hasbeen
in the eyes of the transparent community?

Wherever it came from, it bloodysundayed his nut
rioting like a losthishead soldier through his brain.
It wanted to take him over yes the sad
    bastard it wanted to take him over.
                    Around the room it buzzed.
Ace took the black knife of Thomas Street and cut
its throat. It jerked, died. It would never possess him, never.

Will *never* ever be a buzzword? Ever?

Buzzword in the mud

Some irrational lout clouted the buzzword in the eye
and it sank in the mud in Westmoreland Street.
Ace couldn't tell which buzzword it was, so he
stepped forward, bent, peered, plucked it out

of the mud. Poor buzzword! Zoolookered head to toe!
What was it? Accountability? Re-engineering?
Transparency? Performance indicator? Down sizing?
The more Ace kept peering

the less he saw. He said, 'Fuck this for a lark'
walked down the street to O'Connell Bridge
threw the buzzword in the outgoing tide.

Did the buzzword drown? Not on your nanny!
It rose up out of a pre-dictionary urge,
unmudded, shook itself, looked around for a clear head,

found one, candid woman, lodged itself there.
Someday soon, it'll tumble head-over-heels in the unregulated air,
bee's wing, starlight, curse, firebrand, love-act, knife, gossamer.

A word of praise

Darkening evening; O'Connell Bridge;
Ace de Horner saw a word of praise
float down the Liffey towards the sea.
Never in all his deepbewildered days

had he seen anything so fragile-beautiful.
Was it, in fact, moving there at all? Or was it
the shadow of a tiny bird fluttering in his head?
Yes, it was there, minimal, exquisite,

slipping out to sea from the rumour-machine town
where against all the gods it was born
but could not live although it might return

some future time after a growing spell in
the dangerous, nourishing world elsewhere
to battle in the city of toxic communion.

God's laughter

Someone had mercy on language
changed it into something else I can touch
I can touch
          grow to love, murmured Ace
as he heard the stranger talking of how
laughter comes from God.

Who, hearing words from his own mouth
and from others, can stop himself
laughing or freezing in terror

at sound bubbling up out of infinite
emptiness? Well, fill it with pride
and let vanity strut along for the ride.

When the ride peters out at the edge
of small daring, that other sound
opens.

          This is the sound of God's laughter,
like nothing on earth, it fills
earth from grave to mountain-top,
lingers there a while, then like a great
bird spreading its wings for home or somewhere
like home,
          heads out into silence,
gentle and endless, longing to understand

children, killers of children, killers. Mercy. Silence. Sound.
Mercy. Sound. Word. Sound. Change, there must be
change. There is. Say flesh. Say love. Say dust.
Say laughter. Who will call the fled bird back?
Stand. Kneel. Curse. Pray. Give us this day
our daily laughter. Let it show the way.
Thank God someone has mercy
on the words we find we must say.

Druggie

'You're drugged,' she said, 'drugged by words
that laugh at you from one
end of the year to the other, you are
a laughing-stock of language, I laugh
to think you're using words when words
are using you more than
       the needle uses Buck Nolan
       or the bottle Jack Mullane.
          D'you know that?'

Ace listened, grumpypuss, listened, said nothing.

      'You've no words now,' she said,
'No words when you might tell a truth.
But I don't blame you, druggie, cos
you're hooked on giddy little yokes
that laugh at you.'

Defeated by the Simplex Crossword
      Ace drooled into his tea
         ruminating
on these unwritten lines about children
         dying from cancer
because of the changed nature of the Irish Sea.

Fair play to Ace!

Is it possible to hang a language
on an ancient public scaffold?
Ace dreamed this execution.
He bloodboiled

to see the words of poems he loved
as child and man (half-man?) being
hanged by the neck.
And all the gazing folk agreed

chanting, 'We'd rather be dumb! We'd rather be dumb!
Hang every bloody word we know!
Only silence is true!'

The hanged language was taken down,
coffined, carted away, buried in a remote valley.
Out of the grave, impatient flowers grew,

asking for names. Fair play to Ace!
He named every flower in that distant place.
Once named, the flowers were calm and still.
They loved their names. They do. They always will

while Ace, sometimes, in a corky mood,
stands, sniffs the air. Thank God for flowers' gratitude.

Performer

If only he could perform himself for an hour,
for a minute itself, Ace knew
he'd scale the laughing heights of power,
scale himself in his true

ultimacy. That sounds like an advanced
disease but is the reward of the performer
becoming what he says or seems to say
to the audience in some theatre

of his mind: these people are cruel and kind
and ready to listen. Listen. OK. Ace is speaking
words he has stolen from his dreams,
he's going beyond the doubt he always finds
in daylight words, he's not using them, they're lifting
him out of his distrust, old griefs and shames,
they're shaping him, giving him the form he
never had, investing him with dignity
lost to the world, he's innocent again
and will be till he's forced by decent claims
of men and women to mutilate
himself, his words; to be, once more, hurt, adequate,
articulate as any punter in the gaming pit.

Under a sign

After bombing the ex-policeman's house, the two men
    drove to Dublin, joking
here and there along the way.
    A good laugh shortens the journey.
        In the city
they coffeed at a table under a sign that said
    'Thank you for not smoking.'

Search

hymn
   litany
      dirge
         panegyric –

                    the shrieking chorus of seagulls
circling the tractor driven by a man
whose wife cries in an otherwise
silent house

                    will be a story
told here when horny old Kerr
sticks his prick into Kitty Bannister

             and a child is born
                    to gather it all together
                         in
                              a
                         fabulous
                              epic
             in search of a name

Old bags

Look at him there on the stage, knees
wobbly, eyes older than the pyramids,
voice without an age.

'Listen to the old bags, will ya!' says Janey Mary,
'You'd swear he believes he's from another world.
Ah well, so long as they don't lock him up!'

She listens as he words on and on,
boring her to giggles. She's amused, more
than amused at Ace trying to open another door.

But she lets him do it because that's what he's for
even when he looks the pure eejit and doesn't care.

The river he would become

I'm a river, Ace said, and I passed myself out
a long way back. That was the day I said
poetry has a life of its own, of that there's no doubt,

and why shouldn't it enjoy that life, be it sad
or happy, as much as any man or woman dares
enjoy his or hers? The question leaped from my head

like a boy from a river's bank on a summer's day,
swimming towards a rock that seemed miles away,
a land as distant as the tantalising stars

winking like older boys who know so much more than he
would ever; yet the day will come when he, returning
from the city, will see the rock a few simple strokes away,

so near he wonders how once it set him burning
with adventure, so far beyond his reach in the river
where he must wade and watch, learning

to kill eels, tickle trout, see shadows bend and stretch
in colours he'd no words for but admired with all
his heart, the same heart that would cavil and bitch,

envy and evilspin, love and yearn to protect and nourish while
the river failed in memory but not in fact, making
its seaward way in the old implacable style

he dreamed of, longed for, worked for in the shaping
times when praise and blame were blessedly unknown
and he could walk the streets or sit alone, pondering

the life that had the right to breathe in its own
way, not his, yet he followed words climbing walls of cathedrals
and pubs, dancing, shuffling with or against the grain

of his mind creating and coping with its own trials
twisting like eels in his days' deepening river,
making signs like crosses, bells, branches, clouds, wheels,

the river he would become, moving, moving there, here, here,
there,
directed always, directed through a blinding somewhere.

Real cool

One heart-chilling night
Ace, wrapped in his IRA trenchcoat,
wrote a poem.

It impressed him.

He looked at it from side to side,
up and down, in and out,
many times.

Reverence
soaked his every sense
including the sixth, seventh and eighth.

This is it, he said, this is light,
winged and holy, bee's knees, best
words in the best order, McCoy,
the full shillin'.

A week later he looked at the poem again.
His eyes darkened. All signs of joy
vanished.

'Did I write that?' he asked, 'Am I
guilty of that post-human rubbish?'

'You are,' the poem said.
'You are, God help me.'

Ace de Horner chopped off his head
with his black Thomas Street knife,
opened the door,
kicked his head
into the street.

'Cool,' the poem said, 'real cool.
I hope you two never again meet.'

Barney Hanley

The Wicklow bus pulls in, pulls out again.
The Bank of Ireland might be Mount Tabor
if my mind were a different light.
There are two nails on the floor
where a ladder, property of F. Worthington,
leans against a wall.
In the streets of Dublin tonight
I hear the name Barney Hanley repeated,
repeated. Barney Hanley. Barney Hanley.

Why am I so lonely?

A cheeky lot

If, like so many of your friends, he has gone
into the world of light or universe of dark,
    how do you remember him?
Making his own journey through hell?
Cracking up
at one of his own atrocious puns?
Repeating, at the most telling moments,
the one sentence
he lifted from Demosthenes
whom he also claims as a distant cousin
on his mother's side,
a woman of coppernossity and function
and luciferian pride.

        There are other ways, of course,
and doubtless you'll find him popping up
in your heart or sleep or conversation
when you least expect him
as if darkness and rot
had never existed.
Dying is a lousy business.
The dead are a cheeky lot.

Occupation

Ace dream-occupies his enemies until they occupy him.
This occupied man
explores the roots of the original mistake
causing him to chart the cold destruction
of poisoned milk
ramping
Sinnegans Lake.

On the mark

Ace strolled by the Liffey.
A seagull shat on his head.
Janey Mary's laughter poured over him too.
'Ah, you're covered in good luck,' she said.

Facing faces

'You're a tripper in bed,' sighed Ace,
'Zipping through me like a silken fairy.
You've the face of an angel,' he moaned.

'And you've a face like a slapped arse,' said Janey Mary.

Don't blame

'Don't blame an old man,' he said, 'if he tries
    to acknowledge a girl's beauty.'
'Don't blame a girl,' she replied, 'if she drives
    a knife in an old man's belly.'

Obedience

'What're you doing, darling?' she asked.
    'Rhyming,' he replied.
'Lay your head on my innocent tit,' she commanded.
    He did. He nearly died.

Skittering home

What do I care what they think of me?
I do what I do and I let it go
while a duck skitters home to rest in the Liffey
a bit up in the air with the April snow.

The morning star

rises, shining child of delight.
Whose daddy was shot dead in Ranelagh last night?

Did he blush?

'I was slammed in business,' he said, 'and in my
   personal life,
I'd to pay a million of the best to get
   a new wife,
      then the door slammed shut
for a while
     and I learned that
I was the toughest, meanest piece of shit
     in the world,
I didn't crawl in to a corner, stick my finger
     in my mouth
and say "I wanna go home". No.
The day I knew I was a mean shit was when
     I knew I was someone.
     But tell me this, fella.
what are poets like when it comes to the push?'

Ace de Horner slammed shut like a window in winter.
     Did he blush?

It will be

It will be a darkness deeper than you've known
  since you were lost in that cave
where you floundered, stumbled and waited for the sea
    to be your grave.

It will be a light brighter than has been seen
  since the sun lit the wet blade of the plough
driven by a man in a field outside a town
    unpeopled now.

Zoomuse

Ace saw poets behind bars

sprawled, prowling, electric-tense, all slack.
           He stood and he watched
   a slow, meandering fly
     on a tiger's back.

Dublin truth

'Is it true,' said the rubadub Dub to Ace,
        'that you once
        screwed a Sister of Mercy
        who was so on fire
        with frustration

        she screamed

        as you laid her on the floor
        of your Bluebell pad

        "You are my salvation!"'?'

The rubadub Dub grinned, grinned.

        'Is it true? Is it true?
        Tell me! Tell me!'

Ace de Horner wiped his home-movie brow:

        'No,' he said, 'it isn't true.
Or it wasn't before you asked that question.

        But it is now!'

Vomic drama

What passion dare equal their cannibal fuck
after the bell of midnight struck?
And what indifference could ever be
cosmic as hers; his, subsequently?

Stars are laughing in the sky
at the vomic drama they espy.
Although their cool critique is free
what is their judgment to you and me

daybedding some book of poetry?

Rings

Watching three youngsters
(rings in their noses, rings in their ears)
beat up a tourist
at the corner of Merrion Square
                Ace de Horner
thought he'd like to join the standing Army,
learn how to fight and, if necessary, kill.
                Instead, he shouted
                at the youngsters
                who turned
                looked
                laughed
and beat him up as well.
Recovering, Ace joined the recovered tourist,
                shook hands
                said 'Welcome to Dublin'
                and shambled off
                for a few beers
                        ignoring
                as he walked
                        all youngsters
(rings in their noses, rings in their ears).

Match

That night, all night, she screamed into his skull.
  Dawn saw her quiet, all spent, at peace.
He rose, looking for a word, found it,
  and with it, small release.

Return

when you think it's gone
it returns
for good, for bad,

like a smell from a laneway
a window opening after a congested night
a quick drink

to animate the sound of footsteps
voices circling before they stab
an engine starting up

like a spent runner coughing
determined to run one good race
before he must drop

Whore

'An honest man vainlabours days and nights
to strike a line that may endure
but the Muse is whore
and sleeps with shites.'

> Janey Mary read this in bed.
> 'So do I,' she said.

Generation map

The years, working in ways he couldn't see,
       blindwrinkled Ace.
One day, a four-year-old boy
       looked at him and said
       'Why are there
          so many roads
             running up and down
               your face?'

Ace oldsmiled.
       'Must be the traffic,' he replied,
touching his skin. 'See what the traffic does to roads.'

> The four-year-old seemed satisfied.

A source

'Life is performance and I
am a poor performer,' wrinkled Ace,
sitting on his recent pile.

'Evil is boring and I'm a bore,' he noted.

Once he got the knife in himself, however,
there spread over his craggy mug
a slow, pacific smile.

Crime passing

The three old bombers sit at table after dinner
           sipping brandy in a best hotel.
Time was they'd blow it up for demons to drink
           blood in screaming hell.

But crime passes. And brandy grows on a man.
           Talk, as well.

Lost place

Wouldn't it be nice to have a wee cottage
in Wicklow or Connemara
where I could go and meditate
on the sheer evil of Dublin

but dammit I'm part of the evil scene
as I watch the magpies rise
to the topmost branch of a winter tree
defining the horizon.

The country has come to the city
and will never again escape
to its pure pagan grandeur.
Civilisation is rape

and as we rape each other
with our tongues minds eyes
we have plans for our children.
We'll make 'em classy, rich, wise

as a guy with a black leather bag
at a traffic lights, a phone to his ear
airwaving the present, structuring the future.
There's nothing to fear

but this odd eruptive desire
for a cottage in a lost place
with silence for a strolling companion
and a clean wind in your face.

Whether I follow a wall splitting twenty fields
or sit in a rattling house by the sea
there are many things I have to say to silence.
Silence has many things to say to me.

Proverb

At the front gate of Trinity College
Ace reads the proverb in a morning spit:
the heart of man is empty
and full of shit.

Half-way

Would you believe my eyes
almost hurt with disbelief
when I saw
in a field half-way
between Listowel and Lixnaw
a scarecrow
in a mini-skirt?

The greatest moments

'Why is it,' mused Ace, 'that even the greatest moments of love
have a dippy kinship with shit and piss?'
'So that,' said Janey Mary, 'you won't be losing the
                                    run of yourself
when love turns to whip the shine off your bliss.'

A tickle

Janey Mary eyes Ace and Kanooce, the words
    of an unnamed serving girl tickling her brain:
        'When a woman has tasted a dog
            she will never want a man again.'

Janey Mary's eyes giggle at man and beast
    trudging through judge-for-yourself Dublin rain.

The greatest Irish poets since Yeats

'It is my considered view,'
      said a criticfriend to Ace,
         'that you
are the greatest Irish poet since Yeats.
      The fates
have ordained this happy fact.'

'The greatest Irish poet since Yeats?'
      mused Ace
      his face
a bewildered map of a lost country
    where the rivers have no names
      till we confer them.

'But there have been so many greatest
Irish poets since Yeats,' said Ace,
      including Polly Tickle
            Mother Girth
            Artie Licker
            Alec Smart
            Ginnie Gender
            Colleen Strickneen
            Claire Galway

Eddie Puss
    Bob Scene
        Eithne Mount
           Allie Looya
              Kerry North
                Fanny McErrig
                    Gráinne Wayling
              Louis Flute
            Iggy Noard
        Johnny Cox
      Mona Boare
    Sally Kebabs

and Grapevine Smiley, the breakthru baby.'

'O never mind,' said his criticfriend,
      'You are the man
      in the Parnassian van.
      I have said it.'

'Thank you,' said Ace,
glimpsing the drunken horsemen of Ben Bulben
galloping through the age,
        the horses' manes
having fun in the light
        like a poem saddled with names,
flinging them about with feeling,
        twenty-one helium balloons
                dancing
                on a birthday ceiling.

Two Dubs on Yeats

'Greatest poet since Daly's cat fell down the well!'

'Pity the bugger couldn't spell.'

Heavy

Ace lifted the book.
It was heavy as a house
or an inescapable presence
or pain after nightmare
or the blunt sun in sick eyes

threatening to blind him
or make him wise.

The mirror's advice

Let Harley's barb bite into your heart,
    recalling all you've lost.
Look in the mirror, take its advice; laughter,
    laughter at any cost.

The most evil man

The most evil man I know
forbids his children to sing,
                    plays Mozart
backwards,
                bids you listen
                and says
'That is the true thing.'

On or off it's knock or scoff

'He's off the drink.'

                'Christ! What a bore!'

'He's back on the drink.'

                'Dangerous fucker!'

The art of pinning

Pinned by Janey Mary
Ace looked unto his heart like de Valera
    in the bedroom's icy weather
and said 'the horror of separation
outweighs the crime of being together.'

'Aren't you the philosophical ould bollocks,' she replied,
    pinning the poet against the bedroom wall.
'Sleeping with you is an experiment in absurdity.
    Why do I bother my arse with you at all?
If I release you now, rag doll, will you fall?'

Survivors

Clouds
    like frightened girls
        run through Dublin skies.
Undaunted birds of Spring are having a go
        in trees, survivors
                of ice and wind and snow,
a world packed with starving cries.

        Ace de Horner
        sits in the dark,
        pain in his eyes.

3

**Holy Mary, mother of God,
plant a laugh in this poor sod.**

Like a bleedin' prophet

Warrior Kanooce despatched his victims
with ferocity and skill.
God spoke to men, not pitbulls, saying
'Thou shalt not kill.'

And yet Kanooce the killer is a lover too.
He's good for Ace, good for poetry.
Last week, Kanooce was in a fight.
He won the fight and lost an eye

to a maddened kinsdog from Inchicore
which ate Kanooce's eye before
Kanooce ate him. Now, the one eye in Kanooce's head

gives him a weird look, as if he saw
more with that one eye than most humans
do with two. Like a bleedin' prophet, as the man said.

When a god's scars are many and deep

Is there a new sadness in one-eyed Kanooce?
Not because he sees less but senses more
of the city's laced-mutton squalor?
Dare I suggest Kanooce is getting older

(oh yes he still fights and kills with all
        his pre-pagan ferocity
but you'd be hard put to count his scars now
        and his one eye,

moon of murder, reddens and blackens like a light
fighting with itself).

                Nobody can say
he looks dejected

                but is he sad?

What difference do all the killings
make? Bearing deep scars, what may one say?

                    A man or a woman ages into grey.
Kanooce is ripped and mauled
              but he can still go mad.

Kanooce is two rivers meeting. For miles and ages
each has flowed as it had to flow.
They meet. They're one. Locked and fluent, they move

Together. What is this new river? Only gods of the river know
who in their silence have their scars too.
When a god's scars are many and deep, something is true.

That accurate moment

Blood-constant Ace searches for the word for the sea.
If he finds it he may tell me.
If he tells me I know I won't forget.
Here's to Ace, the sea, the word. I may hear it yet.
I dream of that accurate moment, the time
I may know what word is my home.

Love-letters

'My heart is all yours, love,' de Horner wrote
to Janey Mary, one morning cold and wet.
'Darling,' she replied, 'I accept the gift of your heart.
I may have it for breakfast yet.'

Agony Aunt

Worried by the piggery of his heart and language
Ace wrote to his favourite Agony Aunt
in a popular English newspaper
explaining why his words were bearing the brunt
of a honking bestiality he could no longer
control though he tried, he tried.
He explained how these words mucked him awake all night,
he wanted to be honest, all honest, he'd lied
long enough, lies worked, but now he'd prefer shite
in his mouth to lies in his heart.
Yet his truth as he knew it in recent times
had spawned a reeking, rampallian art
(give no examples) and stank of crime. Might
his Agony Aunt tell him how to clean up his act
or must he scribble forever
like one of his mad famine ancestors
whose words were, let's face them, a grotesque fever
boiling in old songs poems tales prophecies,
war-crazed voices in fields and caves,
shagged castles like beggars at street-corners
and proud descendants of nobody dancing on graves.

And all this filtered through a manpig's language!
'Dear Ace de Horner,' replied his Agony Aunt
'Your letter leaves me quite speechless. I don't
know what to say. I could whisper or rant
or pretend I know the cause of your problem
but your approach to language leaves me very sad.
Good-bye, dear Ace, you may have a mind like a sty
but you're not, I believe, at heart, a bad lad'.

Ace drank each consoling cliché like hot whiskey
with cloves, knowing his struggle had only begun.
Choosing a small herd of piggywiggy words for company
he arsed forth for a chinwag with the noonday sun.

What the sun suggested to Ace is simply out of the question.

After

After a night of ridicule and scoff
Ace embraced the nakedness of the poem
the moment it took its clothes off.

The final crime

Give it up, the clock said, give it up now.
No more poetry.

What'll I do instead?

Here's a hammer, the clock said,
take it in your hand,
look around, choose a head.

Not yet, said Ace, not yet.

The clock smiled. I'll wait, it said,
I'll wait, there's plenty time.

Ace looked at the clock.
You have a head, he said, a handsome head.

You could hammer me till I drop, said the clock,
and I'll still be ticking.

Tick for me, said Ace, please tick for me.

I'll tick for you, said the clock,
for the time being.

Time being what it is, said Ace,
that may be for a long time.

The clock ticked like the grass at Ballyseedy Cross
or a brothel in Hiroshima. It said,

A long time? Yes. Until
the beginning of the final crime.

The last of the cheese

In the cool corner of the supermarket
the blue-rinsed pig grabs the last of the cheese
with such ferocity
Ace wishes himself buried
in the courteous ground.
    And he understands
the patient pleasure of the assassin
the blooding of greyhounds
the gruesome legends out of Bosnia
the final terrible silence of Ezra Pound.

The eyes of God

Hot summer night. Janey Mary stripped naked in Saint Augustine Street.
'Jesus, Mary and Joseph, woman!' exploded Ace, 'You're daft!'
'My bum is beautiful, my breasts are firm, my belly's neat
and aren't we all naked in the eyes of God?' she laughed.

Earth-gazer

Ace, on the moon, raised a dazzled eye
and saw a full earth brilliant in the sky.
If he were a young lover again he knew
his love, gazing at that earth, must be forever true.

Outline

Ace looks at the seagull's shit on the window-pane,
finds the outline of the head
of an unfashionably contemplative man

while another slender shitdrop, inches away,

is a knife
saying more than he
would ever dare to say.

Friends

Mirrored, Ace considers his own carcass,
        sighs, smiles, laughs and says
'How withered-sad you look, old servant,
        old scraggy bag o' flesh and bones,
        old stinking friend.

You are me and I am you and we are left
        with each other in the end.
        What more can a body say?'

Ace puts on his clothes, takes a glass of whiskey
        and Kanooces the Bluebell Way.

There's killing and killing the body in it, he thinks,
as he tries the streets of nowhere-home,
who knows what demon created guilt
and rage and shame?

This sleeping, waking carcase is mine
and Ace de Horner is my name.

Prayer for Ace

Hail Mary, full of grace,
light a smile in Ace's face.

Holy Mary, mother of God,
plant a laugh in this poor sod.

Asleep

Janey Mary falls asleep
sitting in her chair
her hair resting on her right shoulder
Bluebell freedom in her hair
guaranteeing when she wakes
a lively time for Ace de Horner
so he sits and looks at her
sits and looks at her.

, once,

Shambling through the parody of parodies
        Ace Amergin de Horner
    dives into a box of Bewley's
        handmade chocolates,
          savouring

        Marzipan Pistachio,
Cherry Kirsch,   Walnut Whirl,
Brandy Truffle,   Coconut Caramel,
Praline Ballotin,   Vanilla Heart,

                              until
            a gluttonous shadow bestrides his back
                        like a cross
                  made of too much
                        goodness
                  in his gut.
            Exhausted, he sits down
                  two thousand years ago,
                        hungry again
                        and eats
                  bits of bread and fish passed around
                        in a steaming place.
            He looks into tired faces
                  and sees
                  Dublin
                  in the rain,
            Dubs heading home
            for something to eat.
            Hunger is what they listen to,
                  its voice is strong, clear, hard to beat
                  and can be heard
                        like a lark or blackbird
                        in Fairview Park
                  where youngsters murdered
                        a lone homosexual
                        one summer night
                        eight years ago.
            Murder is commonplace now, is it not,
                  yet a small part of our thought.
            Tomorrow's killings will cancel out today's.
                  There was a time
            atrocity shocked us into awe
                  but now –

well, Bewley's handmade chocolate is a wondrous thing,
            enough to make Ace break
            into a hum of gratitude
                  even as he sees
                  blood on the head
                  of an old man lying
                  in Westmoreland Street
                  and a motor-bike flying
                  into the future
                  over O'Connell Bridge.

Marzipan Pistachio, Brandy Truffle, Cherry Kirsch, Walnut Whirl,
Praline Ballotin, Vanilla Heart, Coconut Caramel,

> names of clouds
> with large overdrafts of rain
> above the Bank of Ireland,
> angels pissing down
> on this parody of a parody
> of something
> briefly real, once,
> in Dublin town.

The very stuff of poesy

The porter at the gate recalls
drunken nights making young men mad
and old gods frown.
From rage and weariness and Jack MacIlvanney
Ace plucks the knowledge
if a man is born to be hanged
he'll never drown.

Pissed at the twisted outpost

of Europe staggered Ace, dark night
of the eyes and heart. Lost. Nowhere.
Outpost, where he lives, losing sight.
If he knew where love comes from, he'd go there,
but who in hell knows that? Goodnight,
> my love,
> goodnight.

Stage

the drink is a killer
the taxmen are watching
not a tosser for Christmas
de Horner is dancing

landlord is knocking
pub is demanding
doctor is angry
de Horner is dancing

he glimpsed it this morning
the soul's empty retching
on three thousand dead
and more for the hammer

a youngster gunned down
in front of his mother
a sister must witness
the crush of her brother

starved children dying
politicos shuffling
wild youngsters dreaming
in seas that keep rolling

through nightmare and waking
and raped women whimpering
ferocious jets roaring
over small houses trembling

O who dreamed that ever
there might be an answer?
on the stage of no-knowing
de Horner is dancing.

From the Bluebell Nutbook

In the intensely aroused lover, wrote Ace
                in the Bluebell Nutbook,
sexuality and metaphysics tend to overlap.
He brooded on this till he felt slightly sick.
                For the first time in his life
                he knew in his heart he was
                    a thoughtful prick.

Days

She said 'I got caught in a downpour yesterday
and it suddenly struck me, drenched,
I am never happier
than when I am with you.
That realisation, however, may have had to do
with the effect on my head of sudden drenching rain
so I don't want you to take it as gospel.

Today, I'm enjoying a modest September sun,
warm beginning of the Fall.
On such a day, I must admit,
I don't miss you at all.'

The biting life

One night, Ace de Horner dreamed he was a badger
with the kind of bite
which, applied to any of God's creatures,
puts out the light
that may once have been the light of heaven
illuminating the shadiest corners of celestial places

begetting a special radiance in every line
of angelic, that is to say, potentially
demonic faces.
And in his dream de Horner was amazed
to find himself in a ring with dear Kanooce.
Faces of the order mentioned above
spectated the fight.

Ace de Horner, mauling like a crazed poet
   horning for a prize,
      gobbled Kanooce
       jawed him
          chewed him
             mashed him
put out his light.

When Ace awoke he was exhausted.
Kanooce was crazyfresh after a dreamless night.
He sniffed his weary master, anarchic with appetite,
never brighter, never sniffier in all his biting life.

Must be bad

Kanooce dreams too. He has dreams like old buttons
old shirts old radios old socks old clocks old pens
old figures who enjoy navigating positions
in brothels and opium dens.

Unlike de Horner, Kanooce chews his dreams
as if they were the choicest dogfood
in this island of fake silences and real screams.
When he chews his dreams Kanooce feels good.

But there's one dream he can't feel good about.
At the gates of hell he meets another pitbullterrier
with two heads, six legs and countless fangs
chewing the souls of the dead.

This munching horror tries to chew Kanooce
but our hero turns, scuttles hell-for-leather
out of hell. This dream is locked in his head,
causing him at times to whimper like a child.
Imagine Kanooce whimpering! That's wild, man, wild,
wilder than any dream you or I have ever had.

Kanooce fears nothing but this dream. Must be bad.

A furious Inquisition

Kanooce ate a sheep under The Five Lamps in
    the once-bombed North Strand
While Ace de Horner looked on, making
    sounds of approval.
The sheep was a gentle beast slouching
    towards Dublin
To be slaughtered. Kanooce was hauled up before
    the Mutton Tribunal.

> *O Dublin lawyers are a witty lot*
> *And stack their cash in the family pot.*

Forty-five lawyers from Foxrock and
    Mount Merrion (The Rise)
Turned eyes and tongues on Kanooce and subjected him
    to a ferocious Inquisition.
Several made personal remarks about his
    murderous gob (all flies)
While others commented disparagingly on
    his pitbullish disposition.

> *O Dublin lawyers are a witty lot*
> *And stack their cash in the family pot.*

The three judges looked on, dreaming of
    light in Greece
And sun in Spain with oodles of
    brandy and wine.
Kanooce's nose twitched. Christ! What a
    Liffey-sniffing creep!

In spite of all the judges and lawyers
    Kanooce went free,
Pitbulling out of the Four Courts, Ace de
    Horner at his side,
Whistling to a storm of journalists, 'My love
    is like a white, white sheep!'

O Dublin lawyers are a witty lot
And stash their cash in the family pot.

'In this happy land,' sang Ace de Horner
    'this happy land
    of buy and sell,
a generous judge
    a generous poet
        a generous journalist
            a generous dog
will never go to hell,
            to hell,
                no sir,
a generous dog will never go to hell!'

Pique of the weak

Last week, Ace de Horner
in a fit of pique
accused Kanooce:

            'Child-chewer!
            Sheep-eater!
            Shite-sniffer!
            Mangler of your own kind!
            Biter of old men's corpses!
            Drinker of blood!
            Licker of Bird's Custard!
            Mad dog! Creature
            of savage rage!
            Get over to the other side of the page!'

Kanooce barked in answer:

'Fuck off, you subsidised bastard!
Tax-free bloodsucker!
Pathetic little rhyming fucker!
You think your art is divine; mine is diviner.
I only bark what's true.
So fuck you!
And if you have friends in China
fuck 'em too!'

A quiet coffee

Late December, frostiest night of the year,
4.30 a.m.
Next door, a girl is screaming
'Fuck me! O fuck me, David! Please, please fuck me!'
      I get up and go to the window.
The stars are lovers' faces.
      An ambulance starts screaming.
With screaming here
      and screaming there
I scratch the what's left of my hair
and fix an early coffee.
She's still screaming 'Fuck me, David!'
David is humping and hawping
like a frog with arthritis.
David does not sound happy.
I sit and thank the silent lovers of heaven
for a quiet coffee.

PC

'Your prick is Protestant,' she said.
'Your cunt is Catholic,' he sighed
'And one and true and holy'.
She laughed, 'I need converting badly'.

246

Nothing can be proved

belief in God is love
of that frosty December blueness
some people know
does not exist

A cool style

She went to Switzerland because nothing made sense.
Mrs Ladrose, a renowned gifted lesbian,
helped her to confront herself at the Conference.
                    Now she's back in Dublin
sitting in Bruscar Tame's pub in Flip Street
telling a story of buggery and rape
in a cool style. She likes her whiskey neat.
    'It's not simply a question of escape,'
she says, 'It's more a problem of seeing
oneself as a foot, a hand, an eye.
That's how I survived the shock.'
She tells of rapes of her body, her being.
I see no reason why the sky doesn't collapse and cry.
Then she describes a fistfuck.

Legendary

People don't make money; money makes people,
thought Ace, observing the fat man
appropriating the guests seated at table
in the white house within reach of the ocean.

The fat man outlined his philosophy
sticking up like a knife from a deprived childhood.
He was, in his own eyes, legendary.
The guests, bored or awestruck, gazed on the god.

It's just as well Kanooce isn't here
I believe he'd eat the fat man
nor leave a morsel of that white trash behind.

Dogma spread and stank like stale beer
yet they lapped it up. The god drank the wine
of himself, at home in his pyramidal mind.

Understanding

'That night, I understood the nature of crime.
I hit her the second time
because I hit her the first time.'

Responsibility

Out of the freezing dark
these words from killing faces:
We apologise for blowing
your son to pieces.

Ice on the road to Bangor
cracks into stricken voices.

Suffering

False god suffers from constipation.
Hard though he fights it
he could try the cures of five continents
and still not shit.

When these savage attacks of gut-stagnation
hit him, his eyes grow bitter and dull,
his teeth gnash like traffic on Christmas Eve.
His tongue is unspeakable.

False god has friends everywhere
including the medical profession.
Wise doctors attend him with skill and passion.
They try everything, including magic and quackery.
Finally, false god's bowels move and he
shits money as though 'twere going out of fashion.

Relieved, false god leaves a trail of money in his wake.
Men kill each other for it. False god laughs at that.
He always laughs at men who murder for his shit
and as he laughs he goes on making it.

His own style

Ace de Horner depends on Kanooce
yet doesn't always treat the creature
as Kanooce might desire. Life, says Ace, is full of knocks.
When Ace acts the poet he's a bit of a bollocks

and a condescending bore,
his words soaked in self-importance,
his IRA trenchcoat bulging with vanity.
        He thinks his platitudes are wit.
        He's a pompous shit.

Perhaps this vulgar moment is the time to enquire
                Is it possible for
                a simple pitbullterrier
to start a fire?
We shall never know the answer to that one
                but on a cold Monday morning
after a Sabbath expounding his dreary
                intellectual crap
in a style designed to inspire
                a torrent of death-wishes
de Horner woke to find his library in ashes
and Kanooce considering the scene
brooding, you'd swear, on what once had been,
a primitive glow of gratitude in his eyes.

May a bookless man, once book-burdened, ever be wise?

de Horner interpreted the dog's look as sadness
and reflected that his dear friend,
mere pitbullterrier, ugly lump of a beast,
was, in this hour of immeasurable loss,
                sensitive and cool
        unlike many a human fool.

No poet, critic, scholar, Arts Officer
                or scientist can tell
if a pitbullterrier is able to smile.
Weep he may. Growl he must. But dare he smile?

Kanooce gives nothing away. He has his own style.

I wish the same could be said of us all.

Street-corner

'Why do I love you?' whispered Ace de Horner
into Kanooce's cocky left ear
as they stood at a street-corner
while the traffic rattled by.

'I love you because, unlike myself,
you take shit from no one.
You see the innocence in some adults,
the malice in some children.
You bite what you don't like
and sometimes you bite what you like.
I love you because you put the fear of God
into passers-by. I love you
because you're the ugliest joe in the world
with inexplicable moments of beauty
that quite outshine my poetry.
I love you because you hate Chinese food
and traffic-lights. I love you
because you have no mercy
on any fly or flea
you discover on your person.
But most of all, Kanooce, I love you
because you're tax-free.'

Kanooce's left ear twitched. He looked at Ace.
Suddenly his tongue shot out and up
and licked the poet's face.
In that moment the street-corner
was a loving place.

Tongue

The mirror will not spit at him
or tell him to bury himself.
He looks hard at his tongue.
How long has he used it to mutter with,
swallow his words
coax poems into being
tell lies, half-lies, half-truths?

Stories?

          Only stories remain of most
of the people he's known, spoken to,
drunk with, laughed with, left
to flounder in their ways as he in his.

Stories.

His tongue can tell them
with a relish like young love exploring
young love burning to be known to the roots
of its open fire reaching towards the farthest
headlands of desire.
                    His tongue.
He's seen it black, red, pink, white
and colours beyond words.
It continues to work, to ease
words into the air
between him and people
him and Janey Mary
him and dogs and cats and trees and traffic-lights,
him and Kanooce.

His tongue makes love in its way,
its oddbod way, but a way nevertheless.
His tongue can curse or bless
or waver as if wishing to wait and see.
It can choose.
It can master silence.
It is happy to be free.

There are times he fears its freedom,
he chops it
but his tongue recovers, it
heals itself, there it is, ready
and willing to whisper or lash again.

To comfort friend and stranger. Anyone.

It has whipping power second to none.
It makes things bleed, it licks the blood,
is satisfied for a while.

It whispers, a gifted whisper, soft and cool
as a breeze off the sea on a hot summer day,
it whispers music and courage and endurance,
it praises like an angel-choir,
it praises the grass growing
the Liffey flowing
children laughing
young woman crying because she has escaped
                    from her cage,

it praises resolute flowers born of rage,
it praises love that is calm and kind and
hard-working,
the risk of night,
the challenge of morning.

Sometimes it hides in its own cage
keeping itself to itself
hiding, waiting, alone.
Will it ever rouse itself again?

It wants to serve something, somebody.
There are times it knows
nothing, nobody is worth serving.
It shuts itself in its cage.
It freezes.
It sends waves of ice to the brain.

It waits, waits.

One day, it speaks again.

It is a lethal thing.

It is a difficult, attentive thing.

It is aching to say a word
that will help a stranger to say
a word that will help a stranger
to help a stranger.

This is hard to do.

Ace looks in the mirror.
He knows one thing is true.
He knows what is hard to do.

He knows nothing else
but this one thing he knows
in the blood bone pulse

of being.
Is this why he believes
the greatest achievement
is a moment when one
stranger is kind
to another?

Is this
his true way of seeing?

Is this
why he is going blind?

In a prophetic mood

'You're kind,' she said, 'so I'll tell you
why I shall live longer than my man
who pays serious attention to his pain.
If I can afford it
I get my hair done,
put on a bit of make-up
and meet a friend
not to start talking
of my pains and aches
awful complaints
old mistakes
but to have a laugh and try to forget
all creatures and forces
in me and about me
that may hasten my end.'

The drunken sea

We made our way by the winter sea.
The knives are out for you, he said.
    The sea was tumbling drunkenly
    I felt the knives above my head
My heart danced at the thought of blood.

I saw a man with rotten teeth
   Scrounge for words to make a blade.
I heard another cursing youth
   And every youthful escapade.
The dancing knives sharpened my head.

I looked into the drunken sea
And saw the bright knives dancing there.
   Flecks of foam borne on the wind
   Were bloodflecks playing in my hair.
Be wakeful as the wind, they said. The knives are here.

Biffos

'I slept with a Biffo last night,' she said,
'A big ignorant fucker from Offaly.'

'And what was the Biffo like?'
'Better than a cold doorway.'

'Are there many Biffos in Dublin?'
'Enough to keep a lost woman warm.'

'And where do you meet Biffos, my dear?'
'Everywhere.'

A tolerant dog

Kanooce is a tolerant dog.
He puts up with his own kind
more mercifully than most poets do,
confronted with the work of other neuro–creative–tic minds.
      He'll turn a benign eye on a greyhound
as if admiring a tested warrior,
he'll throw a quizzical glance at a swanning collie
and is fond of almost any terrier.

But mother of God in highest heaven
how may one explain the change in Kanooce
when he sees a poodle pranking down a street?

One leap from Kanooce, the poodle is gone,
lost in the swamps of Kanooce's bellyjuice.

       Is Kanooce satisfied? Certainly not.

Is the poodle's life of groomed privilege
the reason for Kanooce's devouring rage?
Why does he wishwash every feature
of this refinèd, perky creature?
Why does the wee harmless thing make him so
ferocious?
      Nobody claims to know,
   nobody will speculate publicly
   on this aspect of Kanooce's psyche.

A challenging walk

Ace finished his tin of Bachelor Beans
and began to nibble at recent dreams.
Nothing came of it. So now it seems he's
the most foolish man in the world.
He can live with that.

His foolishness extends like the road to the far West.
That'd be a challenging walk.
He might chance it sometime.
Who can say
what a spotty bollocks might meet along the way?

256

Irish poets can't think

'I must think,' said Ace, 'I really must think.
I met a man with a B.A. who said
Irish poets can't think, they merely sing
in their chosen brand of ink.

This much I know: thought is a bird
trying to sing, O there I go again,
thought is a bird trying to sing when a hard
wind clatters its throat and batters its wings.

I must learn to fly with that bird.
I must learn to let myself rule the sky.'

   Kanooce sat listening patiently.
Then he bit a chunk of *The Oxford English Dictionary*
(volume eleven), and chewed it happily.
Indeed, as Ace in wonder noted, thoughtfully.

Plodder

Kanooce sees the politician
emerging from the Dáil
stroll down Kildare Street.
The politician is a smile
aimed at anyone.
Kanooce plods behind.
God knows what's in
the politician's or Kanooce's mind.
God sees a politician and a plodding beast
defining a Dublin street.
The politician pauses
at the entrance to Flower's Hotel.
Pauses. He's about to dignify the place.
He smiles. Kanooce opens his jaws,
volcanoes, eats the smile
off the politician's face.

Kanooce the plodder vanishes without a trace.

Fascist?

'That Kanooce is a fascist dog,'
muttered Ace de Horner to his psyche,
'But he supports me, he supports me.'

'Take him for a stroll through the wildest bog
in Offaly,' suggested the psyche, 'he might
love the open spaces, freshest of fresh air.
If Kanooce is to discover a healthy gentleness
surely it is there, at the heart of the goodness of nature.
Free him from Dublin's babbling poisons.'

So off to Offaly with Ace and Kanooce
and into the bog, storied bog, nothing but bog
as far as eye of man or dog could see.

Deep in the bog, Kanooce starts to dig.
He unbogs four corpses, one headless, in an hour. Ace
whips him back to Dublin in a hurry.

Is Kanooce a fascist? Wait and see.
Back home, Ace, breathless, snarls: 'Fuck you, psyche,
for advising me and my supportive dog
to risk fresh air in that murder-cluttered bog!'

Psyche cowers, cringes, craves release
in unpolluted, deep, decapitated peace.

Her giggling toes

Ace gets very emotional at times and kisses
Kanooce's ferocious gob while giving
the dog's body a number of rhythmical caresses
that prove this battered poet is still living
        while others whisper 'He's past it! Past it!
A joke whose early verse promised much, delivered little.'
        Now, he prowls the streets, muttering 'Blast it! Blast it!

Let me write the lines that show me in my fettle,
let me fulfil that nimble, youngman promise
when all agreed I was a rising star.'
   Gutted with doubt,
   Ace bends to kiss Kanooce.
There's something odd about these kisses.
A grown man embracing a pitbullterrier!
And yet, who knows what'll come of it? Who knows?

Winter kisses its last leaf, summer its first rose.
My old lips have kissed her giggling toes.

Ifology

Ace de Horner eyes the infinite white page
he'll stain with words, flipping tricks of ink.
'What can I say of ignorance hatred rage?'
he asks himself, 'And how in hell do I know what I think?
How far can I go? How far will I go?
Dare I push it? Or just play? Play? Play safe?'

The questions bob in his head like corks
in a floodgutter. He moves into his world of If.

Ifology is soon his forked concern,
people are ifs, Dublin a capital If,
the if-mountain grows, Ace continues to climb,
he looks at Kanooce, the dog is made of scorn,
his eyes say, turn the mountain into a cliff,
jump into the sea, be a criminal of rhyme,
write like I bark, write like I bite,
mix my fangjuice with your timid ink.

Ace listens, picks another if, chews it
sagely. Ah yes, this is the way to think.

Lines

I'd a decent line in my head this morning
said Ace, but it vanished when a man
approached me without warning,
clapped me on the back, laughed, was gone
like my line. Where do these lines, born
of a loneliness otherwise unspeakable,
vanish to? Are lines lonely as men
and women? Do they, too, suffer some private hell?

Why the hell am I talking to you like this,
Kanooce? What do you know of loneliness,
poor pitbullgurrier, hornmad beast, ugly joe?'

Kanooce let out a howl that cracked a glass
on the kitchen table. Ace looked in his eyes,
his head half-split with lines only the old gods know.

Another night

Ace opened his eyes, liberated the radio
for news of last night's killings
(he'd miss that tittle for a start to his day).
On they came; bombings, muggings, robbings
empowering Ace to face the light
of the world of men in which he told himself
he lived, yes, this is living, the night
with its mares and stallions slipped down the gulf,
it will never come again, that night, the next will be
different though the same in ways.
                                   His eyes
x-ray the Bluebell pad, he sees where he is,
(of how many men may this be said?),
Kanooce under the table, words buzzing like angry bees
from Ace's dreams, he'll find the right words for the cries,
if he can't, are his dreams all lies?

He'll wonder all day long whose was that face
accosting him in the pitiless freezing street,
swanny neck, lips plumed up and wet,
young woman, beautifulsneering at his side.
Such are his people whom in dreams he meets,
has met, will again, cannot name, yet must, before he can face another night.

Blue frost

'The blue frost of Christ
   settles on my skin
as it settles on every bare bough.
   Look at me. Is sin
   freezing to death in me,
   corpsed beyond where and why and how?
May I not laugh and love and grow again
   like decent women and men?
Let the blue frost live in me now.'

   Ace chiselled his desire
and heaped black Offaly turf on the fire.

Clearing the way

In the chatty sky over Dublin
         three clouds trip each other up
           in haste to clear the way
              for the cocky Bluebell moon.

Attitude to a repeated question

A posh bad man from Upper
Glenageary wanted to make
Kanooce come a cropper
because our hero had, not by mistake,
eaten the posh bad man's good wife's poodle.
So the posh bad man arranged to shoot Kanooce
in a wicked small shed
        on the banks of the Poddle,
    a river
    not held in deep esteem
    by your average, gut-the-fuckers Dubliner.
The posh bad man lured Kanooce to what looked like his doom
and pointed a rifle at him. Kanooce bit the rifle
because to Kanooce in his banks-of-the-Poddle mood
that rifle was a mere trifle.

Then he ate some of the flesh and drank some of the blood
of the malignant gentleman from Upper Glenageary.
    Somehow, they both
    reached home,
    the man diminished,
the dog contented though leg-weary.

The good wife went to work on her diminished man.
Ace de Horner caressed Kanooce with
'Tch! Tch! Where have you been? Where have you been?'

Kanooce never answers a repeated question.

Hard to beat a good book

Now and then, as if against his will
and his experience of himself and his world,
Ace de Horner wonders who is the real
poet – himself or Kanooce?

              (The arrogant myth
              behind the question
              is a Liffey rat, to begin with.)
                    Yet why does he wonder
this? Why should the question arise?
Kanooce, after all, is but a supportive dog,
a lump of bestial company in the dark days
when men and women are stains on a rug
in front of a fire always going out.
    And yet, there he lies, sleeping, not killing,
resting not fighting
a friend not a threat
              but all these in one,
              contained, a battleground
somewhere in history, a town, hill, field, lake,
hackings, stabbings, guttings, voices pleading
for water or mercy, neither to be found,
all jammed into this beast that for poetry's sake
puts other creatures, and himself, in danger of bleeding.

Continue reading. And whatever you do or say
                    don't give the game away.

Ashes of old poems will sing

Scribbling and scribbling in the deepening mire
Ace de Horner accumulates manuscripts
at a crazy rate. As they rise higher and higher
              he rifles his wisdom and wit
to find how he may get rid of them.
O the stink of old poems! The painful stink!
    Here goes! Ace dumps a lump in the fire,
poems burn, he watches, flames make him think,
he starts to write, more paper is stained
with tears of dreams, screaming thoughts,
longings.
              They enter the fire
lightly, lightly, as if on wings,
the fire begins to burn into his brain,
the poems are there engraved, he'll have to burn
himself before the scribblings are extinguished forever,

before there is an end to yearning.
   Even then, after all the burning,
   ashes of old poems will sing
               drifting, drifting
here, there, anywhere
               on the scaffolding air.

Another voice

Ace de Horner, knowing that poets are snoopy
bastards, loves to listen to heartbeats, tongues, including
his own (such colours!) going from laughy-laughy
to weepy-weepy in one brief morning
or evening not to mention horrors erupting
in the atrocious peace of midnight when
accusing ghosts dionysiac his nut
using the language of wronged women and men
chewing each other (sex or famine? bit o' both?) in some prison.

               What is there to do?
How may he respond to voices that see
through him?
               He eavesdrops on himself, boldly.

   He is a gasp, a curse, a sweat, a tortured frown.

Then another voice shoots up through
               all the voices, urging calmlycoldly:
'Write it down, you snivelling bastard, write it down!'

Good blood

Mother Girth said, 'It's best to be political,
the truth makes people suffer, it brings pain.'
Though it was raining, Ace took Kanooce for a walk.
Kanooce ate a poodle in the rain
and licked his lips, good blood, like one true
sentence in an otherwise trashy review.

Mother Girth is bleeding

The Mother of all poets, Mother Girth
is bleeding
in a small upstairs room
in Ballyflab Parish Hall
        (where during the Emergency
        old soldiers had a ball
        and Sergeant Callaghan
        put Tilly Sullivan up the pole)
after a poetry reading.
Mother Girth's colleague, Ace de Horner,
climbs the stairs
with Kanooce, no foolish airs, lumping behind.
Though Mother Girth's body is bleeding
there's ice in her mind.

Kanooce begins to lap her blood on the floor.
'I hate that dog,' she says, 'If I could stab him
I'd feel blessed.'

Ace says nothing, Mother Girth's tongue, he thinks,
is like the knife
that pierced the side of Christ.
What happened that knife?
Or was it a sword
sharp as a word?

The thought is gone soon as come
and serves only
to emphasise the glory
of Mother Girth coming into her kingdom
amid poetry and blood
and orgasmic probings of good and evil
in a town where praise
is sometimes lavished on drivel
and vomit poured
in rare oul' style

on something worthwhile.

Licked

Despondent Mother Girth trudged into the hills
above Dublin in the icy January light
(half the streets were dug up because of gas failure,
        Nazi Signs
    fought with anti-Nazi signs
    in the Dame Street night):
Mother Girth lugged her flesh out of this
scene so starved of metamorphosis
into the failure of her magic potions,
the failure of her pills and spells.
        (Such ignored loneliness down there.)
        Up in the hills
far from the spare consolation of her skills
she lay tucked under a bushy rock.
        Kanooce came to her there
like a clumsy lumpy god of good luck.

        Mother Girth felt sick.
When she saw Kanooce she said
        'I hate you.
But if you lick me back to life
        I won't poemcurse you.'

    Under the bushy rock, Kanooce licked her
as she'd never been licked before
in bed or laneway, on hill or shore.
A warmth invaded her out of the icy light
and tided her body from head to foot,
her spells returned with singing vigour,
gunwoman now, quick on the trigger,
she'd a bag of myths
no longer sick,
her legends laughed, her rhythms ticked over
kickstarting her words, there was hope of a lover
        in the icy light,
        the light of ice.

        Down
        she came
to her city of gossiping shame,
        venomous, fluent tongues
        electric with poxy wrongs.

Alive,
she was feeling alive,
alive, alive-o.

Now she could bear
the sight of the signs,
Nazi, anti-Nazi,
in the Dame Street night.

And she didn't waste
time wondering
how long she would last
till her future was past

but was ready
to give it a blast

though her mind and heart
faced the ancient problem:

how do I start?

Cauldron

Mother Girth squats in a corner, splitting a hair,
myths on her skin like sweat-drops in summer,
her body the sun with B.O., her head a fat moon
unmoved when the clumsy youngsters drown

in each other, his hands exploring her,
a country exhausting an avid adventurer.
The hair splits in two, Mother Girth smiles,
her head a cauldron of magical syllables.

Café Caruso

Though it was a ludicrous suggestion
she might have overlooked the absurdity
or at least pretended to agree
were it not that just then
a trickle of fried brie
wandered from his mouth
to the tip of his chin
and stuck there
for all to see.

Trolleyed

Ace de Horner, struck down by
an attack of what they dub depression
– one snake one monkey in either eye –
rattled by the old division
between body and mind, the recurring insoluble folly
of breathing endless ignorance, was ambul-
anced heehawing to Idiots and Lunatics Hospital
and arranged in a corridor on a trolley

for five nights while monkey and snake
(who'd never mistake each other
for being other than what they were,
precision-bombing being the essence of their characters),
conversed with him in cool, hideous familiarity
of money smells poems ulcers flu January holidays God

until de Horner, refusing to be trolleyed anymore,

resurrected, clothed himself, staggered through Dublin
to find Kanooce waiting in the Bluebell pad.

Kanooce licked Ace's eyes as he sepulchred into bed.
Five spiders conspired above his head. Body and mind
linked tentative hands in the land of the dead.

Listener

Ace listened to her blur-wording all night long,
   her sleep cawing with rooky loneliness.
Then she spoke a steely, quivering line.
   Ace inclined into her darkness
      and drank her wine.

Discovery

One icy night
I found this pen in a rainy street.
What will it write?

Country butter

Ace is very fond of country butter
but recently in Galway when he tried
to get it, he was told that an order
from a Brussels Bureaucrat prevented
country butter being made anywhere
in Ireland. Not healthy, the Bureaucrat said.
Ace flew Kanooce to Brussels, who entered
your man's office and bit his head
off.
   Back in Dublin with the goods in a bag
Ace held a funeral reception for the head
in a musical chapel in Glasnevin
Cemetery. In a brief but touching oration
he revealed that country butter was back
on the market and the Bureaucrat safe in heaven
where, doubtless, much work remained to be done.
A tough job. But heaven had found its man.
With or without his head, he's king o' the scene.

A moment, an eternity

           Ace
           made
the sign   of the
           cross

on himself.
As he did so
his own evil
welled up in
his heart like
the stormy tide
that'd frightened
him most
as a child.

He was paralysed
a moment
an eternity
but he unfroze
and stood
and walked towards
the Five Lamps
and the crossroads
    there.
As he walked
his step grew lighter
and he rejoiced
at the rain that fell
like a blessing
on his clobbered hair.
He took this to be
a good sign, well,
as good as you're
likely to find
anywhere.

Like breathing

Thirty years ago you lied about me
  in your calm style.
Since then I distrust trustworthy men
  with a budgeting smile.

And yet you forced my own lies through my mind
  for which, much thanks,
and also for suggesting that the truth may come
  from madmen, saints and cranks.

I'm not sure. (There's your smile once more.)
  Are lies like breathing to us men?
Now and then a woman cuts me to the bone.
  I think again.

The unthinkable

'No television! No television!' roared Ace,
  'in my Bluebell pad!
Suppose one night I were to see myself?
  – O God!'

The violence of questions

As he walked out of the prison
questions locked themselves in Ace's head,
walking street after street, road after road.

Why does my head move in the Unisex Hair Salon?
Why does the gull mangle the ball of white paper and ignore the girl
    scattering bread?

Why does the fat man beg me for 'anything, anything, a bit o' change,'
        with vomit on his lips?
Who wore the red cap pitched in the gutter?
Why do women swear by Cod Liver Oil pills?
Who is the man smiling at me under the Reduced Fat Sunflower Spread?
When did I last say a prayer for the dead?
Why do these three men look like killers in the blue muddy van?
Where is the Son of Man?
Who thought of monuments?
What is not for sale?
If I'd a face like a telephone would you use me quietly, fairly, obscenely?
Would you pay for me?
Would there be a record of what you said through me?
Do trees growing together for hundreds of years ever get to know each other?
What is an oak tree's favourite weather?
Why do I move?
Whatever prompted me to leave the safe stupor of bed this morning?
Why, after forty years, do I hear Henry O'Donnell roaring in agony in the
        football-field, the Clounmacon full-back having given him a deliberate
        kick in the balls?
What was the source of Annie Taylor's modesty when she stripped to her
        petticoat and aged sixty-three slipped into the barrel that took her
        over Niagara Falls?
Why do I want to say the word 'cold' over and over and over?
Is the sun a fascist?
Why do so many muttering Irishmen support Hitler who's alive and well?
Do sped souls dream of wrecked houses, bits of bedrooms open to the sky?
Who made love in rooms that are now gaping spaces where a seagull's cries
        flutter in like letters I'll read and never answer?
Is a walk into freedom an invitation to danger?
Why do some folk prefer to die and call it living?
Did the moon recoil from that first human touch?
Would I walk on the moon with an old lady hampered by a broken ankle,
        old lady willing to try a walking-stick but too vain to try a crutch?
Why do I feel homeless passing the Happy Home Design Centre?
How many drains in my bodyspirit are blocked?
Why is one for sorrow, two for joy, three for a girl, four for a boy?
Should I get a bell for Kanooce's neck?
Would I agree with the spoofer who said that the slipperiest villain on earth
        is a man's prick?
If the graves of Dublin opened, and the dead walked the streets, what would
        the living look like?
Do letters love or hate numbers?
Do Pam and Mandy really love Cooper and Canty?
Would I win the title of Ultimate Slut?
Why do I hear the sound of hooves in the headbanging traffic?

Why do I say aloud, never talk to me of madness until I see you naked and
     ready in all your bushy glory, repeat that, several times if necessary?
How did that crow's shit, dropped from a considerable height and with
     professional detachment, miss me?
Who is Saint John of God?
Why are you looking at me?
Why am I looking at you?
Are you blind as I am?

The questions were hammer-blows in Ace's head.
He must walk beyond this violence.
He tried, he tried,
walking street after street, road after road
till the day died

but the questions didn't die

nor will they ever.

Will a cool mind define a fever?

What is mercy?

Ace ruminated: most days I'm reasonably bright
if a shade morose, somewhat arthritic yet
sharp, resourceful, capable of exquisite
effects (by accident, mostly) but

                    am I credible?

How can I tell if I'm credible?
Do you find me credible? Will readers find
me credible (fuck 'em if they don't, that's secret) or will
they say I'm a bore, slithery, vain and blind?

Will they say I'm a genuine pain in the ass,
a deluded wimp, a dedicated wet
past all believing?

Or is there something in the nature of my art
(ahem!) which defines me as a complete
fraud whose major skill lies in shapely deceiving?

I'm at your mercy, not for the first time.
What is mercy? Show me. I mean no harm.
I love the gentle rain, the blackbird, the worm.

Front Gate

I met Ace de Horner at the Front Gate
of Trinity College. He was looking out
for Kennelly. 'Why are you looking for him?'
I asked. 'Because the bastard makes me dumb
with anger at times,' said Ace, 'and I'd like
to give him a bloody good piece o' me mind.
I'm in the right mood for that. It's time to strike
a blow.' 'Why bother?' I said, 'sure he's only a fat
bollocks at the best o' times. You'd see him there
arsing like an ape across Front Square,
a big smile on his foolish face.
He used to be a fuckin' disgrace
in the old days, a hoor for the drink,
he'd floor whiskey out of a hole in the road.
As for being an academic, sure the man can't think.
Why did they ever let him in there, in the name o' God?
It used to be a mortal sin to go to Trinity College
without the Archbishop's permission,
but that little fucker is uglier than any mortal sin.'

'I'll tell you this,' said Ace, 'he's a cute Kerry hoor,
he'll go in a swingdoor behind you, and before
you know where you are, he's out in front o' you.
He'd get in where the wind would turn back!
Why don't they give the bastard the sack?'

'What do you think of his poetry?' I asked.

'Bad, black, blasphemous rubbish,' Ace replied,
'published by these Bloodaxe Bastards in Newcastle upon Tyne.
There's one thing sure! They'll never publish mine!'

'They tell me Kennelly was married once,' I said.
'But the drunken bollocks went clean out of his head
and his wife, a decent woman, a fine, tall,
intelligent woman towering head and shoulders over that small
knacker, threw him out. She was too good for him.
Of that there is no doubt.'

'Not only that,' said Ace, 'I hear he's a womanising prick,
he'd ride a cracked saucer in the thick
of a storm, he'd screw a poxy cat
miaowing through a skylight like a wounded
lyricist of the Celtic Twilight, he'd tip
a midge in a mist,
quarter, half or totally pissed.'

'I see,' I said, 'that's helpful to know.
But he's arrogant and vain also.
He's foolish, too, if you know what I mean.
He advertises Toyota cars
and the little bollocks can't even drive!
I mean, did you ever see such crap in your life?
Is there a poet among us with such an under-
developed sense of the ridiculous?
Jesus, it'd make you wonder!'

Ace de Horner stood between the statues
of Oliver Goldsmith and Edmund Burke.
He gestured aloft, right and left, and said
in obvious pain, deeply aesthetic pain:
'To think that such men
came out of Trinity College, and see
what it produces today.
A fucking car-salesman
pretending to be a poet!
Do you know what?
I'm glad I haven't met him!
If I did, I'd cut the balls off him!'

'Mr de Horner,' I said, 'Don't work yourself up.
A major poet like you
should have nothing to do
with a venal wretch like Kennelly.
It's better to calm down and go your way.'

Between Burke and Goldsmith, Ace
stood, statue-like, all passion, honour and grace.
'Yes,' he said, 'yes, how right you are.
A true poet must follow his own star
though it lure him
into the damned heart of eternity.
I think I'll walk out to Sandymount strand
and stroll by the buttock-loosening sea.
Yes. To ease my soul, that's what I'll do.'

He started to move, halted, turned.

'By the way,' he asked, 'who are you?'

'Me?' I replied. 'Nobody. I'm just passing through.'

Same reason, I'd say, the blackbird sings

Over the years, Ace, in the midst
of conversations that grew passionate
and often burned on into morning,
developed the habit of clutching his bum
firmly, right hand on his right buttock,
left on left. Somehow, this gesture
deepened his intellectual passion
and gave irrefutable authority to his words.
He'd stand there,
perhaps in the middle of O'Connell Street,
clutching his bum as a drowning man
will clutch whatever comes to his assistance.
Ace the bum-clutcher
clever, oracular,
found himself able
to get to grips
with issues that bamboozle us all.
When he was deeply bewildered
he shifted his buttocks
a little farther apart
and began, as it were,

276

to talk through his arse,
revealing his soul
while a wispy tincture of fresh air
rejuvenated his hole.
He looked a bit odd, of course,
but seemed neither to notice nor care,
discoursing on love and politics,
how to face the music, turn bellyflab
into a rockhard stomach in just
seven minutes a day, the clever nature
of the IRA smash-and-grab, the steady
poisoning of the world's fresh air, the role
of poetry in creating the Irish soul,
some differences between artist and charlatan,
how to spot a typical American,
the evils of sealculling and whalekilling,
(but are we getting sentimental, are we
killing enough grey seals and black whales?),
the search for inspiration, our western
speculators ravaging a booming
but corrupt Phnom Penh
and the mystical significance
of Mickey Mouse
for men and women
to whom rodents are icons.
The harder he clutched his bum
the better Ace understood these things.
Why? Same reason, I'd say,
the blackbird sings.

Squeak

A prophetic American poet held that
Republicans and Democrats had died out,
not a Presidential squeak in the White House,
White, so White, inside and out.
Then someone had the happy thought
(I do believe it was a chap called Pratt)
of making Mickey Mouse

the first obvious Rodent President of America.
After all the crooked, futile years
Mickey came to power. Why?

His ears! His ears!

His ears are two indelible black circles,
two ebon halos at the head,
indestructible, growing more and more

    soulful.

Yellow shoes, oval buttons on shorts,
game, basic, bare-chested, imperially undead –
this is the Mickey Americans adore.

'There's a lot of that Mouse in me,' Uncle Pratt said
'But I ain't gonna let that beauty go to mah head.'

Pyjamas

For the New Year
a thousand million
two hundred and seven
Chinese
are going to wear
Mickey Mouse pyjamas
and crawl
from end to end
of the Great Wall
to celebrate
this hero-friend
imported
from America
to right all wrongs,
inspire
a deluge of
popular songs
in honour of Mickey.

One song will ask
what are the consequences
of wearing these
pyjamas?

Tricky.

Rigour

Ace reads the line
   rigorously.
   He sees
Buddha with gold-dust on his shoulders
   tribal eyes
a sprawled cow facing the east
   a poet's greedy letters
masks of comedy and tragedy
   a lonely priest
a street vibrant with menace
angels over the Bank of Ireland
a professor pondering Unit Cost.

Again,
   rigorously,
he reads the line
and begins uneasily to sense
   how little he has found
   how much he has lost.

A curious condition

Sleepless again, Ace sat and brooded.
The Complete Works of William Shakespeare

in a lovingly annotated edition
fell from a shelf on his head
and left him in a curious condition.
He was a bad farmer, bankrupt, prodigal,
a conqueror, afraid to speak, in the grip of shame,
a sixpenny striker among purple-hued malt worms,
false man, true thief, burly clown

              scrounging for a name.

Did he find it? Not on your nanny,
not so long as he wandered through that
lying landscape he called his mind.

His mind cleared, he still felt funny
as he took the big book and caressed it
like a favourite child shining with wondersound.

Would he find the right sound for his unsleeping wound?
Or sit awake forever, darkness all around,
rapist of virgin paper?

Sleep is a fickle hawk, a choosy tinker.

Murderous night

It was a murderous night for Ace.
  He murdered his parents
  his brothers and sisters
  his descendants, all his descendants.

The dream was sour-faced, wore a black cap,
enfeebled him for a whole day,
   his whole body weak as a rush,
   his mind weary

but he upped and staggered on
through word gesture smile.
Where do dreams of terror hide
when the world grows visible?
Why is daylight such a liar,
darkness horrible-truthful?

Or are daylight and darkness of such a kind
Ace is, in either instance,
blind?

Omelette

In such a quiet city, not even the sound
of the usual rain, not even a scrambling
canister to grattle the edges of his mind
like a crowvoice prackling into parodysong,

why did Ace hear, continue to hear
explosions at three and four in the morning?
No longer a man, he'd become an ear
absorbing the thunder of his exploding

city, children blown to smithereens,
public monuments in pieces,
cathedrals and brothels in fragments.

He left his bed, sat, listened. The explosions
continued, became voices and verses
someone somewhere would doubtless call heartfelt.

Memory is what I can't forget,
peace is the absence of truth, he thought.
I think I'll rustle up an omelette.

The problem of placing

How do we place him? How do we place
this grinning Ace with the idiot smile
cavorting all over his travesty face
as he forges his own de Horner style

    with the help of Kanooce

against the odds and gods of the city?
    He's stuck here, that's for sure,
this post-colonial mickeydazzler
in the second city of Empire,

stuck in the dead centre of paralysis,
the womb of rumour vile and vital,
the shitpot, crackpot, nuthouse tomb of love

past all redemption but not analysis.
That's it. He's here to analyse our fatal
gobwobbling. Well, bless his heart and keep him alive

till we decide to kill him off
with a roaring, racking, critical cough.
We'll place him then. How about the Sad
Romantic in his Bluebell Pad?
Or the Blind Wanker
in his trans-Liffey Bunker?
Or the Transcendental Dickhead
scrounging for love like a crust o' bread?
Or the Carnal Mystic of Dublin Seven
whose fleshpoems are steps of light towards heaven
but break in pieces half-way up?

So many labels are available to us
I'm sure we'll do the bugger justice.

After the kick

After the kick in his face
Ace wrote, Grace
is the ability
to go my own way
without being compelled
to use my words
to violate those
who'd kill me.
It's my capacity to ignore
whatever would force
me to murder
and know why
I want killers to live,
not die.

That's what I write.
Do I live it? Like shite.

Don't tell Ace

Don't tell Ace you can explain him
    by a grief
or a beasty teacher beating him
    in a style beyond belief

or random loves in a thousand nights
    of delirium
or daylight nightmares that might suffice
    to strike you dumb.

Don't tell him any such thing or hint at what
to you may seem a proper
explanation of his ways.

Let him dream of Bird's Custard, peppermint,
peace, Geary's Biscuits, lemonade, love, chips in greasy paper,
words that paralyse and praise.

Let the old rag doll go down a byroad in the rain,
pluck wet September blackberries
from briars twitching in his brain.

Let him bury his past (or try to), resurrect his future
so that he appears to himself
a breathing creature

not heeding those who say he's dead
because they know something that explains
certain cold rhythms in his blood,

hells glimpsed by his sleeping eyes,
wrong choices (were they choices?), hurts he inflicted,
angers, self-pitying cries.

How can anyone tell him what he must do?
You try. I try. You get it wrong.
Me too.

To the well

Ace went to the holy well at the back of Lisa's house.
He walked a guttery path and came
to the well surrounded by grass and moss.
It had a certain fame.

He felt her eyes in his back sizing him
up and down through a rear window.
He stood at the well, knelt under a cloud of good luck,
stared into the water, saw himself, depth of his sorrow,

depth of his ignorance of himself and others.
He prayed into the water, it listened with sweet calm,
if he listened long enough it would reply

in its own way concerning his troubles.
He saw the woman's eyes in the water, he turned
towards the house, her eyes guided him on his way.

The well waited, there was always someone wanting to pray.

Beyond all reason

Ace listened to the river
telling a story of
bullets, blood, glory.
He listened to a train
telling a rhythmical tale
of loneliness and pain.
He looked at faces slipping past
and heard centuries singing
of struggle and waste.
He turned to the river again
and for a moment knew
the sympathy it had for men
who poisoned it without a thought or
even a single moment's shame
for the long crimes against water,
not to mention each other.
    If Ace had brothers and sisters
they were these voices
everywhere about him,
within him,
talking to each other.
That's why, for reasons
beyond all reason,
at unlikely times
in unlikely places
and in a style
that amazes himself,
his heart rejoices.

Wink

He smiles at Ace and winks his head
makes clever chortling look-at-me sounds
then hits the road in his faithful van
to collect the dole in five towns,
in Bluebell,
in Athy,
in Kill,
in Celbridge
and in Withershins.

Someone and someone else

Someone insulted someone else's God
in a play a poem a story a book
that electrified the mob's blood
and sent them hooting for revenge. 'Look,'

they cried, 'at what this wretch has written
in these pages blacker than any sin
anyone has ever committed.
We must do the bastard in!'

The scribbler of insults came to Ace
and stayed in the Bluebell pad
calmly, fearfully, not venturing out.

The mob howled. Kanooce licked the scribbler's face
while someone else insulted someone else's God
and fresh striplings of revenge began to sprout.

The smile on the sky's face looks infinite.

Somewhere in Ireland

Strolling with Kanooce in the Phoenix Park
close to the Wellington Monument
where the Pope said Mass
Ace, seeing a rapist at work,
paused dumb with astonishment

a moment or two. Then he said,
pointing his right forefinger, 'Kanooce! Kanooce!'

In the midst of the fifteen hundred acres
Kanooce cut loose,

chomped into the rapist's arse in no time,
then chewed his prick and balls
with Bluebell gusto.
The rapist ran bleeding and howling away.
Ace took the girl to hospital, Kanooce licking her
healingly the while, her name was Margo,
safe now, wept uncontrollably.

Somewhere in Ireland there's a man without balls or prick.
Isn't it enough to make you sick?
On the other hand, this man without prick or balls
may inspire an impressive assortment of satisfied chuckles

since responses to crime and sin
vary
according to the company you're in.

First drops

first drops of rain on the concrete:
    tears of Christ
darkening the Paraclete

Rare

Ace swallowed the insult, then he swallowed
another. He had to admit the man was right.
How could Ace know which path he'd followed?
What moment is all sunlight and no cloud?
Poetry is rare as the grace of God.

Born

At the top of the stairs she stood, opened her legs,
pissed on him. This was something most
women no longer did, or had forgotten how to do.
On this occasion, it worked. He was
        a smelly pissed-on ghost
        of whatever constituted
        his former self,

  his threats limp as used tea-leaves.

She towered over him
        laughing in scorn.

Like herself, he was delighted to be born.

The big print

Ace's eyes are burning:

      will it be half-night forever?

Is that solitary magpie gone?

      Such a bright chap, never heard of again.

It's the big print from now on.

Eye

Ace looked into Kanooce's remaining eye.
　　It was round like the world.
It was sad like Ace's heart.
　　It blinked now and then.
It was sharp enough to enable Kanooce
　　to get his fangs into the flesh
of a few appropriate public men.

It was an eye with stories to tell
leaving it up to yourself to listen badly as well.
It suggested a sea without a name
and anonymous forest-people introduced to martyrdom.
There was something in it
would never be satisfied by anything
but the flesh and bones of those
happy to send others to hell.
Closed in sleep
it seemed always awake,
the kind of eye to profit from even a small mistake.

It said
'Stay on the lookout, bud.'

Ace looked at the eye for hours on end
murmuring, now and then, 'My friend! My friend!'

Now, going blind

For as long as he remembers
　　Ace has seen faces in the fire.
　　　　Now, going blind,
he squats in front of his Bluebell flames
and stares at them in search of faces.
　　　　There's one,
reminds him of Philip Lever
who did seven years in Limerick prison
　　and came out, explosive as ever.

There's another,
the spitting (nearly) image of Scourge Malone
who drank and lied his way through life
and was more loved than any honest man.
          And there's –
no, it's fading, fading. All the faces
are fading now, soon Ace will see
          no more faces
but those he'll conjure from his darkness.
     What are the faces of darkness like?
What happens the faces in the fire?
          He sits and stares,
          the very flames grow distant,
their fingers shaping faces he can no longer see.

     What shall I be in a world without faces?
          A world without your face?

God grant I'll always be a cheeky devil
     claiming that what I see
     in my darkness without end
          is up to me.

Pure music

In that moment the wind stood still.
Pure music lived in the ruins of the old Norman Castle.
Who'll hear it again? Ace will.
Will he enjoy it? With all his umbered soul.

Only a crowd

It is only a crowd
but it swallows Ace
and the worm in his head.
It laughs in his face

when he tries to tell
of the boy out of prison
free in a boat
drifting home.

And the crowd jeers to hear
of the clumsy man loving
the raven-haired woman
and failing, failing.

Now Ace is the fool
jeered by the crowd.
Did he ever think he'd long for
the worm in his head?

The worm eats him as he fades
through streets of midnight
bearing in his blood
the crowd's orgy of spite.

He folds the spite into his heart
like a letter in an envelope.
The worm says, study that for years,
you'll never understand it, and never give up.

Boy crying

The umbrella at his back
is tall as himself. He carries
a rose, uplifted, in his right
hand. His face is tears, all
tears. His murdered father
is nowhere in the picture,
out of it, in front of him.
This is Ireland, kill-and-run
losers believing they've won,
a boy crying forever,
every word that ever lived
corpsed in the noonday sun.

Good at pretending

He's good at pretending he's gentle.
    There are other skills
at which he's known to excel.

Kanooce eyes him in the streets of Bluebell.

Nightduty

'She speaks to me for hours on the phone.
I let her speak, I say little,
    sensing her loss.
She says I'm a mind-fucker. Maybe so.
    She doesn't know
there's a line I will never cross.'

A Bewley's sticky bun

'I would like to share the absolute truth
with you,' the Krishna nun said to Ace
in Bewley's of Grafton Street.

'Thank you, no,' stammered Ace.

'Why not?' she asked.

' 'Twould...'twould...'twould kill me,' he said.

'But you'd die happy,' she smiled.

Ace brightened.

'May I share my absolute truth with you?' he asked.

'What's that?'

'I'd love to love you.'

'I'm a nun!'

'I'm a man.'

'I'm sorry.'

'So am I.'

'Has anything come out of this?' she asked.

'To be absolutely truthful, no,' he replied.

Ace gazed at the radiant nun.

'Have another cup of coffee,' he said,
'and may I interest you
in a Bewley's sticky bun?'

'Never,' she said, 'never,'
and fled.

Next to heaven, they say

What is the dream
   of loving men?
A holy hour
   in the Furry Glen.

Holy Seer

At a gathering of Irish poets in Dumb Cat
Ace de Horner was made a Holy Seer
by the High Queen of Ireland.

Ace was old now, slightly pissed,
a bit of a hard man and a most
distinguished bard.

The High Queen said, 'Ace de Horner
has given his life to poetry,
all his years to the art and craft of verse.'

'Wasn't I the right eejit?' chimed Ace.

The High Queen continued:

'Like all true poets, Ace de Horner is a rebel,
singing out against injustice and evil.
All his instincts are subversive
yet he fills our lives with pleasure.'

         'Subversive, my arse,' spat Ace.

The High Queen smiled and went on:

'As a critic of society, Ace de Horner
has no equal. The man
has a mind like a scalpel.'

'O Christ,' moaned Ace, 'me back is killin' me.
Where's the booze? Gimme a whiskey.
Words are useless! Worse than useless!'

On and on the High Queen rolled:

'Ace de Horner is an example to young and old.
Through all these lonely years
he changed the muck of his experience
into pure gold.'

'O Kanooce! Kanooce! Where are you?
Where are you, my only friend?' groaned Ace.
'Must I go on listening to this crap?
O Jesus Christ, me poor back!'

The High Queen looked around the hall.
The poets of Ireland were gathered there,
a dashing pack, male and female,
sweet singers all
evoking you and me before the Fall
in verse that wouldn't shame the angels.
The poets looked at Ace
and smiled in his face,
the battered map of a country
where he'd always be a stranger
no matter how much he pretended
to be at home there.
Home is where
pretence is the real thing.
Therefore, sing.

'Hell is in Bluebell,' said Ace
and scratched himself.

The poets giggled.

'Why the fuck am I not in Amsterdam?' asked Ace.

And then: 'Maybe I am.'

The High Queen went on:

'Ace de Horner has the courage of the loner.
While others enjoy the warm security of home
or an academic salary with a cottage in Kerry

de Horner stalked the streets
of his own lonely heart
and brought back music to enchant us.'

'I want to die!' moaned Ace,
'Let me outa here!
Let me back to my Bluebell cell.'

The High Queen brought the matter
to a gracious conclusion.
She placed the legendary
Tork from Cork
around Ace's neck
and pronounced him a Holy Seer.

'There you are,' she murmured, 'There you are.'

Ace was now
the only Holy Seer in Ireland.

He hobbled from the hall
cheered by all the poets.

He was a sad figure
as he negotiated
the Main Street of Dumb Cat,
the Tork from Cork around his neck
scavenging for a pub.

He found one, entered, ordered whiskey and beer,
asked the barman:

'What am I doing here?'

The barman was a poet as well,
like every second damned soul
in hell. He said,

'I know you. You're Ace de Horner,
you're the only Holy Seer in Ireland.
You have the Tork from Cork around your neck.
You influenced me as a boy.
I know your poems by heart.
You bring me joy.'

'What am I doing here?' repeated Ace.

'You're the Holy Seer,' said the barman.
'What do you see?'

Ace closed his eyes.

'The old familiar darkness,' he replied.
'I see Kanooce.
I see Janey Mary.
I see the Liffey
and my cell
in Bluebell.'

'You are truly a Holy Seer,' the barman said.
'And may you live to see
happiness stretching from here to eternity.'

Ace killed some whiskey and beer
and wiped his mouth.

'Thank you,' he said, 'Thank you
for telling me why I'm here.
But how do I get to Bluebell
from Dumb Cat?'

'That is a long haul,' said the barman.
'The bus takes four hours or so
and stops at every godforsaken spot
along the way. It's a rough journey
for the Holy Seer, massive potholes,
very bumpy, little or no rest.
The Tork from Cork will be hopping off your chest.'

Ace finished his drink, made ready to go.

'Goodbye,' he said.

'Goodbye,' said the barman. 'D'you know what?
You'll be remembered forever in Dumb Cat.'

Ace looked very tired and puzzled.

'Dumb Cat,' he whispered to himself.
'Dumb Cat. Dumb Cat.'

'Dear Holy Seer,' the barman said,
'May God go with you on your road,
bumpy an' all as it is.'

'Neither God nor I,' said Ace, 'is very fond
of human company
but if He'd like to join me in the bus
from Dumb Cat to Dublin
He's more than welcome.'

And the Holy Seer began
the long slouch towards home.

Cisum

That night with nothing in his head
          Ace took love
and wrote it backwards:
          Evol! Evol!

He walked out beyond the city
          and came to the sea.
He wrote the sea backwards.
          Aes! Aes!

Cisum! Cisum! Where was his music now?
Ti saw enog! Ti saw enog!
The city turned edispu nwod.
Ace's head spun and shook.
Stars were opening like schoolbooks.
If there was a road left he wanted to call it a road.
Or God, it was God.
If worlds are masks, masks must be worn.
How often can Ace endure being born?

One above all

Ace has many pictures in his head
    but one above all
haunts him down the years:
    in the spilling
            rain,
his father, sharp-eyed,
            in some pain,
on hands and knees
            scouring the grass
            for a lost
            shilling.

Gold

At a bend in the Liffey, after much talk,
Janey Mary turned to Ace and said
        'Kiss me!'
    He did as he was told.
        That moment
        and a few others
        constituted
        everything
de Horner recognised as gold.

Things that might silence

Janey Mary said to Ace, 'You're a cripple
and dumb, you're afraid to say whatever
you have to say, I'll say it for you, I'll
say anything in the wide world for you.'

'You will?' he said, 'Why?' 'Because you bore me'
she replied, 'with your long cowardly silences.
I know you want to say that you adore me.
There now, I've said it. Does it make sense?'

'I didn't say it,' he said, 'I said nothing.'
Janey Mary spat in his eye and went home humming.
Ace shrivelled into silence deeper and dumber
than any he'd shrunken into heretofore.

In which condition he could clearly see
and hear things that might silence you and me.

An odd concoction

Ace loves moments bitchy sacred electrical uncouth.
    Ageing, he dreams of wrinkling into youth
and would lift a farthing from the shit of
    the street with his teeth.

Janey Mary calls him an odd concoction
and celebrates his every poetic erection.
Ace sinks deeper and deeper in dereliction.
Will Kanooce help him? Quick, pitbull, quick!
Give your master one redeeming lick!

Year by year

Ace scribbled the years as the years scribbled him.
    Did they give him a style?
Was he a liar who spoke the truth
    or a scrupulous fool
            whose laughter faded
            year by year
            into a thin
                    bitter
                    smile?

Until

Why did Janey Mary
wear black and red yesterday
and refuse to appear today?

Or why did she press on Ace
a photo of herself in her
First Communion dress

and then whip it away
never to show it again?
Janey Mary, the way is pain.

'I could bring the British Empire
down single-handedly but please
never mention my name

in that connection,' whispers the neat
looper in the coffee-shop.
Ace respects his wishes,

gets to his feet, vanishes
to see a gentle
German woman step in a Dublin puddle

and stain herself in a way
she never did at home.
But she'll probably stay

for a year at least,
because this town is 'pleasant as a village,
savage as a wild beast'

and makes a lasting claim on 'a certain kind
of person with a slightly
anarchic cast of mind.'

Is it distress
when the boy playing the flute
finds nothing in his cap

though he's played all morning?
Poverty stoops creeps plays signs begs and is
no shame, but bloody frustrating.

'One crowded hour of glorious life
is worth an age without a name.
Who said that?' asks the traveller

from Sligo, bald and brown.
Ace slips away to a part of town
where there are no quotations

only word of an old friend going blind.
She's still working or trying to,
anything to keep her mind

busy, she's the brightest person
on the terrace, she'll always
have a life of her own

but Ace won't share it.
He's gone already, he glimpsed
a truth and cannot bear it.

For the millionth of a second he
burns through a girl's
fragrant, measureless vanity

to emerge only slightly charred,
glimpsing glimpses of himself,
a scruffy, nervous, wit-and-pun bard

waiting, listening for clues
in streets pubs shops eyes hands
necks buttocks faces voices,

devices to stop him being completely dumb.
Let him nose through all his labyrinths.
Let hints and glimpses come

for as long as they will
until

Small words begin to dance

The Holy Seer is going blind, he taps
Dublin on the shoulder with his stick.
Dublin turns and asks him how he is.
'Going blind,' says Ace, 'blind and bloody sick.'

He hears the Liffey now in ways
he never heard it before.
He leans over the riverwall and listens.
What the poet and the river say to each other

is chronicled by the Four Masters
drowned long ago in the Greally Hole
near Leixlip where the salmon leap
like children's questions in the light.

Tap! Tap! goes Ace beyond Kilmainham
into the holy land of Inchicore.
His bones ache, his mind pains, he sees
Janey Mary standing at her door.

Wasn't God good to give such sparkle to my darling?
Wasn't heaven imaginative and kind
to let me see her standing at her door
this greasy day in Dublin, and me blind,
Kanooce at home, bad-dreaming, growling out of his mind?

Ace taps on into a giftpatch of sunlight
warming his bones with a slow caress.
Could be an angel tickling him for fun
or taptaptap, Janey Mary's kiss.

Tapping through the city, he stops at the Black Lion Inn
in Inchicore, squats, orders a pint of beer,
drinks, is easy, easy. Eyes closed, world gone.
Small words begin to dance for the Holy Seer.

A problem of definition

Art is Promotion, said the Famous Poet.
The first commandment is Promote Thyself,
the second, Demote the Rest.
Ace looked at Kanooce,
     jaws began to twitch,
Ace led him away, locked him up.
Then he sat and pondered
the mystery of past-post-Modern Art.
He farted. He sat and brooded
'mid the timeless perfume of his fart.

The Greally Hole

The pagan Greally came from Clare,
drowned in a hole in the Liffey near Lucan
his cries tormenting the air.
The Four Masters also drowned there.
They knew everything about the island and its people,
a fire waiting to be kindled.
Sometimes, even now, drowned, they sing that knowledge,
 in a hole near Lucan, the Four Masters.
 If we heard them we might learn something
and not be such a shower of wasters
   unhappy
 by the scruffy Liffey
   but one
 with each other and the world,
 the rising and setting sun.

Music lost and found and

The Four Masters, drowned in the Greally Hole,
knew the song of the country, river and city.
For centuries they'd sung it with all
the magic vanished from the world. The story

ran that now and then the Greally Hole
released the voices of the Four Masters
and people heard the lost song for a moment.
Ace, sleepless, sought the Greally Hole, moon and stars

guiding and mocking him. By daylight, also, he
wandered out by Leixlip of the salmon,
questing, questing, never resting, no sign, no sign.
One night, when he'd gone blind, white stick in hand,

tapping his way by the companionable river,
somewhat lost, not caring, Kanooce at his side,
pains in his bones, stimulating as ever,
the Holy Seer stopped, stood rigid. The river flowed,

spoke its own tongues; through and beyond that sound
Ace heard the Four Masters singing their song,
telling their epic tale. Kanooce listened too.
Out of the Greally Hole rose right and wrong,

women crying, children laughing, women loving,
men dying, birdsong Ace had never heard before,
forests protesting at their killing, music beyond wording,
first grass growing, battlecries, hounds savaging each other,
stories in the making, boys and girls dancing through the music.

Where was Ace?

                    Standing there, listening, at home,
out of himself, blind, exiled, belonging. How long did
it last?
    A minute? An hour? All night? It was gone

suddenly, the Greally Hole was silent and nowhere.
Kanooce tugged Ace's trousers. Ace tapped the ground,
shuffled onwards, listening to the river
telling him he was music lost and found

and lost again for someone else to find
by guiding mocking stars, by eyes gone blind.

Once

Before he went blind, once, Ace de Horner
looked into Janey Mary's eyes,
  a nervous boy on the edge of hell
drowned in the light of Paradise,
  a whiff of truth emphasised
  by no more lies, no more lies.

  Ace never forgot that look
as he lived his own unbreakable dark.

Thanks to the mad fires

Janey Mary was the pain in his testicles
the deepest joy his heart had known.
Ace walked through himself in his blindness
as though he were exploring a foreign
city. She might turn up anywhere,
laugh in his face, call him a stupid shite
(which he was, much of the time)
kiss him, say he was kind and bright
(which he could be, some of the time)
a cut above your average hypocrite.
She might laugh, she might cry
but she'd be real as his own blood
keeping him alive, scribbling, thoughtfully sad.
She made his words tremble, rise, dance
and when she said he was a dunce
he took it, knew its truth, pursued her again,
blind old boy driven by the testicle-pain.
When she took his prick in her mouth to suck
he came, and shook and shook
like an old manquake. Old and blind, he grew
to a new man, the old blind thing was new
and stunning as the young sun breaking through
to the quaked earth, look at it, more and more
hills and valleys eyes have never seen before
thanks to the mad fires deep within.
O Janey Mary, love, let love begin.

The house of rage

What can Ace do with the rampant angers of sleep?
Where do they come from? What are their roots?
Who sowed them like a wicked seed?

What turned sleep into a shudder of starving rats
ready to eat the city and the snoozing suburbs
where bricks gossip of slates,

where crime has a growing bloody career
and youngsters maim oldsters for a few devalued pounds
to waste gaily in some kip in their neighbourhood of fear?

No answers, no answers; only the questions increase
in hurly-burly sleep until Ace rises,
his head a mucky field trampled by cattle.

He looks out from his Bluebell pad and sees
Dublin manufacturing one more day of crisis.
He wishes he were in better fettle

but in truth dawnlight is not promising,
the radio is angry, Ace flits from land to land,
nice voices speak a world of rage

bad almost as his own sleep, rages young
and old converge in his throbbing nut,
no, there's no sense, no making sense, there's coffee,

grabby black stuff without which life is
unthinkable, what does it trickywizard in the gut?
He sits, Buddha-still. Angers ring him, an audience

for poems he knows he will never write
because they are brothers and sisters in the house
of rage within the four walls of his mind.

Walls are for breaking through. If only he could find
some way to... the angers quieten, merge with darkness.
He sits in the darkness, calm, enraged and blind.

Walls

'Walls, walls,' said Janey Mary, 'so many walls
to be knocked down.
Come with your sledgehammer in your hand.'
'I'll swing and hit until I drop,' said Ace.
'How else,' she smiled, 'may you hope to understand?'

The radio says three

'It's thrilling when I know how backward I am.
Just listening to folk is enough to prove my stupidity.
The sanity or beauty of what they say fills me with shame
the moment I realise I'd nearly missed it entirely.

Once the shame has passed, however, I'm
glad to be alive.
This greeting of the stupid sharpens the heart.
Amazing how we survive.

Colleen Grove is cursing her parents, calling them
cunts fuckers whores.
The parents have never felt so stupid before,
indoors or outdoors.

But Tom and Molly Grove are learning, learning
from the moods of their druggy-eyed tyrant
who steals their cash from under their noses
and screws the cool bad boys of Ireland.

The main thing is not to give her up for lost
or oneself either, I mean, to admit
that one is hopelessly drowning or
choking to death in a houseful of shit

or brought face to face yet again with the fact
that the language one slogged at is useless
when dealing with a volcanic son's or
daughter's many faces, many voices.

One is lost and getting more lost each day
drifting from those we love as they drift from us
until a man walks away with his own silent cries
responsible, bewildered, anonymous.

I have to leave it like that and wait, wait,
shake hands with my recurring stupidity
surviving the calm horrors, the eyes of others,
the lure of the sea,

wondering who is that blind man with the ferociously
ugly dog I saw this morning, down by the Liffey.
How many people go blind in Ireland every day?
The radio says three.'

Rickety

'Ace, you wheezy rheumatic bag,' sniped Janey Mary
as they cuddled in the rickety Bluebell bed.
'You smell of sad old poems written in blood.'

          'And you,' said Ace,
            getting his nose in deeper,
'reek of the grace of God.'

Two sides

'I'm impotent tonight,' said Ace,
'an erection is what I dream of
    and cannot get.'

'Surprisingly,' said Janey Mary,
'my nipples are erect for you,
    my clit is hot and wet.'

'O would,' said Ace 'it were not so.'

'Right now, for you, you fluke, my juices flow.'

'O no!'

It is time

Ace stared into the grinning Liffey.
At his back, the ruin of Dublin spread
        like a winter pain
through his dreams of living and dead.
He was all right, he was alive and sane
    or half-alive and half-sane
enough to hear himself mutter 'It is time
        to start all over again.'

When the Liffey heard that, its heart beat
like a poet's heart suddenly kicked into life
        in a dying street.

Ace could have kissed the river then
but was content to witness the promise
of new life in the eyes of women and men.

One woman with perfectly shaped bluish
lips approached, looked him straight in the brain
and said 'This could be difficult, this
starting all over again, but I'll give it a shot.'

She would, Ace knew she would. As he drank her
into his heart he saw the faces of many
who most assuredly would not.

So much

So much about Janey Mary I adore, said
Ace to himself, and began to list:
'The crafty way she farts in bed
especially when she's half-pissed;

the way she whispers fuck when I try
my damndest but can't do the trick,
her laugh behind her magic camera
when she photographs my prick;

her freckles in the light of morning
spotting her arms, shoulders, face;
her mirror ways;

her mocking words, sudden singing,
swinging states of shame and grace,
cunt that is beyond all praise,
ice that is colder than the North Pole.

All of which, and more, constitutes her soul.'

Perhapser

Listening yet again to Ace's words
Janey Mary peeped into his mind.
'You are becoming an old perhapser,' she said,
'D'you think you could say something definite for once?'
He shuffled himself like a greasy pack of cards.
'Maybe,' he replied.

Guided tour

'You're the honey of my soul,' sighed Ace to Janey Mary.
'You're my favourite bag o' maggots,' chortled the poet's lady.

Then she gave him a guided tour through some of her no-go
territory.

Culling

'Killing hares is a good idea,'
says the concerned politician.
'Culling, though cruel, is a natural process.'

Kanooce one-eyes six and a half politicians
bullshitting well
in the bar of the Shelbourne Hotel.

Would he cull them?

        Yes,
till there's nothing left but a smell
which suggests that culling
is a necessary process in hell.

This was the will he must wait for now

Between the Liffey and the spot
where Robert Emmett was hanged
Ace stood and listened to the wind

telling stories he hadn't heard before.
He must have been standing there
for the best part of an hour

caged in himself, his galled attention
before his cold body shuffled on,
heavy with stories.

Would he ever tell them to anyone?
Why had the wind so much to say?
If he listened long enough would he go

mad? Maybe the wind bore the dreams
of the dead back to the living
who found it hard to listen?

Then and there, he prayed to the wind to make
him a true listener
that he might hear

stories of those he thought he knew but didn't,
stories drifting unheard.
Would the wind listen to his prayer

or would it turn its back on him,
leave him frozen and dumb
for years to come?

This was the will he must wait for now,
the wind's will that can flourish or vanish,
no reasons given.

On he shuffled
like an old story
impossible to finish

Praise

I will praise your name forever, Janey Mary

    though you haglaugh in my face
    read me like *The Evening Press*
    curse me soon as bless

I will praise your name forever, Janey Mary

    though you gulp me in your stride
    mock my every prick-song word
    abuse me walking Cromwell Road

I will praise your name forever, Janey Mary

    while you sneer at Ace the face
    saying my best is a disgrace
    jibe my bones to nothingness

I will praise your name forever, Janey Mary

    as you ridicule me in bed
    'Think you're living? You're half-dead!
    And your poems are bloody sad!'

I will praise your name forever, Janey Mary

    because praise is right for you
    it's what I will always do
    strive to praise the fiercely true

I will praise your name forever, Janey Mary

Where wolves are kings

Tongues demolish hope in a terminal room.
Wolves are kings of Dublin tonight.
What is human dignity? One old man
sees life as a harvest of light.

A wild iris brightens the Broadford Road.
The wolves, fearful of drowning in the old man's blood,
slink off into the darkness
where curse is the same as bless

but not forever. Did you ever see
a young girl laughing at wolves,
with truant eyes and a roguish kind of ease?
It's enough to make you go on grateful knees.

His forever now

The word came hurtling
out of somewhere at Ace
and cut to a bone

near his heart.
Of all the words he'd heard
this was one of the

smallest and most fragile.
Yet it turned him
into a ghost

of the man he'd been
or seemed to be,
a ghost rocked and dumb

because a friend was lost
forever. Ace touched
the place near his heart

and peered through the years
ahead. Yes, he would
meet him again

but no matter how both
would try to pretend,
the scurvy truth

would make a lie
of their efforts to get in touch.
Maybe they'd meet in a street,

look at each other, begin
to shape some familiar greeting,
'Hello, you old bastard!'

but the words would die
in both their throats
and all because of that one

word.
He'd lie awake at night,
speak to the darkness,

repeat it over and over
in the silence of his mind.
It was his forever now

like pictures from childhood
that came and went
and sank and surfaced in his blood

and swam back into his mind.
His forever, he'd never share it
with anybody. Who was his friend?

Where was the man ousted by the word?
Where was the quiet voice,
the healing laughter?

Drifting through himself like the Liffey
Ace listened to the Trojan river
gossiping to the sea.

How songs escape

There are those who would blast the poor off the face of the earth,
the poor whom Ace meets on his wanderings.
Here is a boy with a shrill scab on his face
in spite of which he sings in the drizzle, he sings

'I never tell a lie, I never tell a lie.'
Ace stops and listens, Kanooce too.
This boy is singing as if he'll never die,
thinks Ace, singing for me and you,

singing for whoever dares to listen.
Someone will win the Lotto tonight
someone is planning to plant more bombs
a woman fondles a stick of gelignite

a journalist urges someone to kill someone else
a diplomat is sorry so many innocents die
Ginnie Lynne is raped at the age of fourteen
and Johnny who raped her knows how to lie

but this boy is singing and it's raining now
never mind, the sun will come laughing out soon
and those who'd blast the poor off the face of the earth
will never succeed, there's a song in the hearts of men

and women sung by the boy in the Dublin rain
that will never allow it to happen.
Ace trundles along with the song, with the pain
of feeling the sunshine fall on the human rotten,

so rotten he cannot begin to imagine
how songs escape the poisonous touch of men
but they do and what's more they flower from that touch
untouched, heart-touching, like promises broken and shaped again.

Nobody has ever heard of poetry

Ace saw all the poems of Ireland
drifting down the Liffey
to drop into the Greally Hole.
The poems joined the cries of anger
                curses of wife-beaters
            writers of anonymous letters
        and the Diaries of the Four Masters.
            Down there
            in the Greally Hole
the verbal music of the island lay
            like dirty underwear
            or drowned puppies
            or hillocks of condoms
after a fab Saturday night in Dublin.
            Down there
            in the Greally Hole
        lay all the shapely dreams
        of certain men and women
            devoted to the craft
that brings the nightmare to its knees
            and weds the penniless seagull
        to the Stock Exchange magpie.

So now
what are we to make
of the drunken poet's knife on the floor
the bloody fingers washed in TCP
the tequila tears adrift in the criminal smile
the beggar more beautiful and bitchy
than anyone who dares to pity her?
And what are we to make
of the pissartist heckling the priest at Mass
the boy who says his life is a study of love
the scandals gulped like unholy communion
the tourists mugged in O'Connell Street
(an' what's the fuckin' Minister for Justice doin' about that?)
the Irish jokes we love to tell against ourselves
(only some o' them are not as funny as the real thing)
because the jokes are true and we are lovers of the truth
and poetry

(truth and poetry my arse!
thank you for the smile).

Think of all that style
lying at the bottom of the Greally Hole
the oldest poets whose names we love forgotten
as well as those whose names are traffic-lights and flowers in hedges
all the dreams of our living chicks
drowned
in the Greally Hole.

Imagine!

Nobody has ever heard of poetry!
Does it matter?
All those Departments of English out of work!
All those reviewers back on the dole!
All those poets who've never heard of metre
rhythm similes metaphors lines.

Not a word has ever been written!

Nobody has ever had the urge
to write anything down!
On white paper!
On white spotless mesmeric paper
waiting to be stained!

Nobody
but Ace,

sly, smelly, sightless, bolloxed Ace de Horner
is putting
pen
to paper

in his Bluebell pad.

And d'you know what?

It ain't half-bad!

(But what'll Janey Mary say
when she drifts that way?)

Ballad tradition

'Take the chair with the cushion,' he said to Ace
    'It'll help your back.'
Ace was a torturer then, merciless, he had this
    gentleman on the rack.

Years later, this gentleman sold his soul
    to a rich lady
with a growing empire and a warty
    infra-structure for a body.

This gentleman dutifully explored all roads
    from skin to bone to breast to brain.
Ace sees him sometimes: an old ballad
    in search of a refrain.

Magpies

Something about magpies Ace loves a lot and fears
a little or loves a little and fears a lot,
that's the kind of bird he's drawn to while youngsters
point at him in the streets with 'The old poet! Old poet!

All on his ownio!'

He feels like one for sorrow
scanning streets and sky for two for joy
or three for a girl and four for a boy o
look at that blackandwhite! Like the mind

of Ireland it is, this or that, them or us
with a subsequent butchery of myth
bleeding to new myth. The whole thing is a story

and we'll be telling it till magpies harmonise
with larks and little tomtits at the window
chirping for bread bringing news nobody can afford

to ignore, but we do, is that why Ace
Amergin de Horner is always on the look-out for something,
some news from heaven to brighten the mug
he turns to the world? Is that what prompts him to sing

his gloomy heart? One for sorrow two for joy
three for a girl four for a boy
Five for silver six for gold
seven for a story that will never be told.

Or will it? Are all the stories a desire
to tell one story nobody will forget?
Ace listens to the river and the people.
One story. He may tell it yet.

All on his ownio.

The bright moment

And what, Ace asked himself as if he were a child
knocking at the door of the house of a man whose name
was dread because 'twas said he was wickedwild
and destroyed young fellas and girls for fun,

is love? Have I known it? Witnessed it?
Stood in its presence? I have, I think
I have (he answered himself) and it was warm
and once I hoped it might express itself in ink

and once I dreamed the Liffey was a river of love
and lovers walked near it, over the bridges
to reach a place they might consider home

and once I heard it whisper in night air,
it was birds' wings making sounds like happiness
when the bright moment came into its kingdom.

Arctic waste

By the Liffey again, he's an
outcast from language now
not fit to jabber with seagulls
let alone humans.
Will words ever return?
Why did they abandon him?
He tries to say
bridge, John, water, Janey, store, Dublin,
but no, he is alone,
more alone than a dead language
or a song that will never be sung again
or a story extinct with the teller.
He is dumb tonight,
even the small prayers of childhood
ice in his throat.
He stands there, waiting,
for what?

Will the ice melt?
Will someone remember the story, the song?
Will the darkness give him
the surprise of a single word?
Will the river speak to him in sleep?
He begins to move through it all,
do not judge him or forget him,
do not say 'The man is sick, I doubt
if he'll recover.'
Let him try to say the seedwords
in the Arctic waste of his mind,
small seedwords like
chance, is, touch, born, Mary, lover.
Let him try to say these, let him taste
the depth and breadth of his Arctic waste.
How long is a frozen eternity?

       Suddenly,
   a word begins to stir,
      to enter him
as if remembering him.
     Blue.
It is growing. *Blue.*
    It is growing.

He shuts his eyes and holds it closer than anything or anyone.
    Blue. Blue.

True.

What was his best?

what was his best
when set against
the body of the three-
year-old boy
murdered in a wood
buried facedown
in a hole,

322

                    but the cry
of a terrified nameless creature in the night
or the whine of his own
heart knowing it would never find a home
no matter how long it beat
how far it travelled
where it might rest
or who it stole comfort
from?

Perry's problem

'Most poets are lazy bastards,' said Perry Winkle,
'too lazy to get out of their own way.
Why should anyone listen to anything
these knackers have to say?'

Partition

'The real partition of Ireland,' said Janey Mary,
'is between those who try their best
and those who don't give a shite.'

Two hundred yards away
a young man shot a young man dead
to prove he was right.

Tongues of fire licked Janey Mary,
her shoulders, bum, belly, breasts;
turned out the light.

Loving his shoulders, buttocks, testicles, mouth,
she burned all borders between them
the long, electric night.

No need to suffer

She sipped her coffee, smiled:

       'That bastard left me
in a state of terrible frustration
but' (she sparkled), 'I'm OK.
I've discovered masturbation.
Myself alone. Sinn Féin. A private art.
No need to suffer the smell of that shagger's fart.'

Over drinks

Who is not a theme?
So many ways to research a scream.
The criminal gets an aura from the crime.
Poet and murderer are serving time
every day of every year.
The Butcher wants Black Bush. Ace goes for beer.

Blight

The ultimate human blight?
People who know they're right.

       The way I say that;
          nifty
      as a Liffey rat

          nosing the mud, the mud,
          the grey, beslubbering mud.

Being humans

The old grey Liffeyrat got in touch with Etáin the shape-changer
and had a go at being humans.

Nipping clear of the mud one promising morning
the old grey rat became a poet for a week
but gave it up
because the job weakened his teeth
and he felt a bit sick being lyrical
among crowds so purposeful and thick.

Next, he was an entrepreneur
and grew to love the magic of lunch
in the Shelbourne
where he often made a killing
between dessert and coffee.

Terrible is the temptation to be happy.

Then he investigated peptic ulcer disease
and foraged for months among hills and valleys
of cayenne pepper and Manuka honey.
He cured an old poet
lying in the gutter
and quit the enterprise,
his days an ever-deepening lust for surprise.

By turns, then, he was a bishop, a sycophant,
a football scumbag, a Senior Civil Servant,
a minor civil servant, a globetrotter,
a biographer, a fortune-teller, a mugger,
a mugged old woman
who kept ninety-seven pounds in a tea-pot
in a cottage (once thatched) two miles outside Carrickmacross
where the sense of history sharpens the sense of loss.

It was fun
being all these, each one
distinctive as a snowflake
falling on Croagh Patrick
in the middle of winter.

But the old grey Liffeyrat went back
to being the old grey Liffeyrat.
Being human was kicks for a while
(thank you, Etáin) but it wasn't quite his style,
not quite his world
              of endless, grey,
                    investigatable mud,
                          fascinating
                                as the mind of God

              or the thought
                    of who will
                          drown tonight.

The bit

The old grey rat flicks through
        the Liffey's muddy pages,
              enjoys what he reads.
Ace de Horner standing on the bridge
        steals from the rat
              the bit
of cheeky wisdom that he badly needs.

The story goes

The story goes that an old grey rat
        ate Nellie Warner's eyes
the night she fell or jumped or was pushed
                into the Liffey.
        Nobody heard her cries.
        Did she raise any cries?
Who saw the rat? Why blame the rat?
        Someone/something must be blamed
              and that is bleedin' that.

What a way to rear seagulls!

In the labyrinth of inveterate punning
show me the mind that
can measure the wisdom and cunning
of the old grey Liffey rat

eyeing the young seagull in the mud.
Young! Well, as old Paul
Herressy said, get 'em young,
treat 'em rough, tell 'em nothin' at all!

What a way to rear seagulls!
To train them for the menticide skies
over Dublin where every bird
better be canny and wise

if it wishes to cope with
those treacherous stretches
between heaven and earth
between wizards and witches!

A bird might do worse
than seek councel from the old
grey Liffey rat navigating
infinite slime, filthy cold

with the sort of patience and skill
denied to most statesman,
diplomats, popes, presidents.
Ace de Horner calls it ratacumen

and Janey Mary says only
poets and rats possess it.
'I don't know what it is,' she adds, 'but whatever
it is, God bless it.'

Janey Mary's bread

'When I make bread I make love,' Janey Mary said,
'And when I see you, early and late,
eating what I've made
you old goat,

I sometimes wonder why
I don't cut your head off
and stick it on a plate.'

Whistling

When the old town is rubbled once more,
back to original mud
and the children of Bluebell and Inchicore
are gone to God
Ace and Janey Mary will ghost the Liffey
seeking the sea
whistling for Kanooce in the cool doggy
reaches of eternity.

Like history

He slaves all day to get the rhythm right
and nearly does
and yet it vanishes
like history in the swindling Liffey light.

Truth is what no poet publishes.

'And small wonder,' pipes Janey Mary.
'Who'd want to read it anyway?'

Scorn

Janey Mary took the rose between her teeth
bit the thorn
laughed in scorn
spitting at Ace's feet
blood of the unborn.

Nourishment

She lifted her head, Ace heard her say,
'Well, that's my protein for today.'

One

he showed them all to Janey Mary

she read in silence
picked out one
said it made these skin-a-Dane March days
like kind words and happy children

I was drunk when I did that, he said

be drunk more often, she replied

  and smiled
      in such a way
          he knew
              he'd never be
                    outcast among outcasts

  even if he found
      he hadn't got
          one word
              to sing or say

The colour

'Kanooce, you fanged snapper!' barked Ace,
    'You'll have the balls and buttocks chewed
        off all our politicians.

    I find you positively lewd!
You disgrace the name of Ace de Horner!
    You disgrace the name of poetry!'

Kanooce smiled, that is, his lips conspired
        to reveal his teeth,
        his overtime teeth.

        The colour of truth.

A voice into his darkness

'You're not a poet,' she said,
'you're not a communicator,
you're a weird old philosopher
           reaching no one.'

        Ace listened,
           listened,
           nodded,
           whitesticked
              on
              alone.

Shadow

In the busty shadow of Molly Malone
            a man roars,
'Let Christianity be abolished
            and Christ restored!'

Ace de Horner and Kanooce stand and listen
            in the town of the Hurdle Ford
taking their places, like guests at a table,
among the damp the tipsy the sober the bored.

Motion passed

'Half-a-loaf is better than no bread,'
hummed Janey Mary, 'and a blind old poet
is better than a freezing bum in bed.'

'I'll second that,' Ace de Horner said.

And still he mutters

Who is this blind old man
(he is old, is he not?)
muttering his ways and wants
in the streets of Dublin?
A girl with dark hair
and kind eyes escapes
through the cracks in his lips.
A venomous killer of names
swims through spittle to freedom.

What's left of a moment of foam
is a block of ice where squats
a tinker turned itinerant
turned thief turned prisoner
turned listener to seagullcackle
in a cool cell. Now
The Mouth is a shortcut to hell,
then a long, straight line.
Look at the blind old man.
Silence every demon
insisting on proclamation
and willing to die for it
given the chance in our town.
They can't keep a blind man down.
Solutions pepper the mutterings,
horror-tales mix with Butthead,
Darwin, Christ, anti-Christ,
here come cartoonists, zine line,
skater dudes, cyberpunk bands,
gangsta rappists, retired rapists,
pro-lifers, papists, anti-papists,
counterfeit satirists, lyric poets hoping
in hope yielding to lipstick,
body piercers, chief executives,
crucial journalists lusting for truth,
last apostles of noble feelings,
pricey whores in denim drag,
sincere apostles of the pure-obscene,
post-Postism, cynics with mortgages,
teachers (God help us)
students (God help us)

and still he mutters
down by the Liffey
through all the pubs
in the gabbing city
staring at churches brothels graveyards nothing
        muttering
for you to hear, you to see

        muttering
words blasted, unborn,
        unrehearsable,
            free.

Seagift

The sea goes out, leaving one
stick, black and bare, in the wet sand,
helpless as logic, perfect as a skeleton

waiting for the touch of a living hand.

Hope

Janey Mary tickled his balls.
His world was bright from pole to pole.
When a man's balls are happy, she said,
there's great hope for the soul.

When you try

by the grace of Ace and his kind of blind

nothing
is worth anything
but poetry
and poetry
is
nothing

when you try to think of

It'll have to do

Dreamers nudge him like remembered books,
whisperings misunderstood at first,
clarified in the last of light.

Real presence is the strangest thing
as if a skin living inside a skin
helped him to grow and see, encouraging.

Not there, of course, and yet most surely there.
There, in the coldest corner of Dublin
stopping him, chatting, moving on

into the eighteenth century before,
the 'dirty nineteenth that produced us all'
maimed and polished us with progress.

Here, a dreamer's voice: a road in the West,
a man hanging sheep in a parish of whiskey,
a virgin swearing she can't know if its cursed or blessed

she is with the men that are going now, watching
her, all wanting the one thing and didn't her
mother warn her to keep the filthy beasts wondering?

The geography of darkness is a map of freedom,
the only thing he reads, while the old legs buckle
and, out of sympathy perhaps, the heart bleeds.

He leaves the drops of blood behind him,
muddles through the town, a legend he
can taste, shuffling up and down,

here and there, hot and cold, so old, so new,
sudden music from a house, a pub, another
dreaming heart, lost, touching false and true

this changing day, not great, not much, the best we have, it'll have to do.

Down

why does a poem
always
go
down
the page
like
a shooting
star
or a spade
cutting
into earth
making way
for seeds
to nestle
in darkness
and slowly
begin
to become
(for example)
a small
white
flower
perfect
in the
light?

A little blood

Ace stumbled over Kanooce
fell on his face in the street,
            began to bleed.
            Kanooce licked him
            till his head
            was a pure clean wound
                  bleeding shyly
like the poetry he'd never write

or the talk of children
discussing what they'd rob
that covering night.

Ace got to his feet
Kanooce at his side
waiting for Ace
to steady himself.
They walked on together,
a little blood between them,
    not much
but enough to suggest

the kind of bond that may survive
states of shame and humiliation
and accusations of being half-alive.

Reflection on howls

As Kanooce bit the mugger
    again and again
Ace, hearing the howls of pain,
    heard himself say
(in relation to a different matter altogether)
    'Repetition is the only way.'

Kanooce hears

Kanooce listens to Ace in the nights when
he laughs, is compelled to remember and grieve.
Ace's words are footsteps crushing crisps.
Kanooce hears like you couldn't believe.

By the ears

Janey Mary grabbed him by the ears and said
'Sweep the caution out of your heart, stand up and sing,
what use to man or God if you're clever and tame-blooded?
Whatever you say, say something
wake-the-dead true, my unopen man.
                    If God had made me a poet
                        I'd thank Him
                                I'd praise Him
                                    I'd thank Him again
                                        and then
I'd fling all the damned shit in the fan!'

Tumbling

Now, in his blind mind, Ace re-writes everything
            he has lived and written,
ways of dreaming failing feeling loving sinning
        while a five-year-old child
            is tumbling
        head over heels from a sofa
        to a cushion on a kitchen floor
        in a house in a town in a country
        where the legends of Saint Nicholas
            and his black Moorish slave
        (Dutch in disguise, sparkling
            rebellion in his eyes)
            assure the children
        the story is just beginning.

An old Ace triad

Ace mindscrawled his triad in the Dublin muck:
See, if you can. Be blind, if you must. And don't give a fuck.
He raised his eyes from the muck to the sky.
Mid-winter. The sun was having a go
though the weatherman prophesied ice and snow.

Hand right hand

sometimes in the bluebell rain
ace de horner considers
concrete walls
while outside
a seagull calls
and he knows he writes
not from beyond the grave
but before the womb

before
after
during

something

running away from him
like frightened love
or loving fright
under moony briars
one september night
when the headlights caught him
then passed on
to leave him like
a child riverdumped
by a terrified girl
with a father waiting

sneer on his lips
shit in his mouth
and
in his hand right hand

a whip

The blindness of poetry

Christ is a tree, God knows
why the theatre-builders
didn't cut it down,

chop it up, lorry it off
through the streets of the town
always game for a laugh.

The topmost twig is so fragile
it laughs at storms,
is friendly with worms

says hello to magpies, crows
and the little nameless birds
constantly vanishing,

turning up like postcards
from nearly forgotten friends
who remember you at the far end

of the earth one night
and reach for the pen.
The topmost twig, the worm's ally,

is the beauty of women and men
and the blindness of poetry.
Nothing dare equal this beauty,

not children, not poetry, not yet,
but women and men. Realised. Blind.
I dare not say this again

because crime is the heart of it,
game traitors abed, begetting us,
incapable of learning from living and dead.

Incapable, I said. Strength realised. Let me say it again.
The blindness of poetry is all
that is wrong with us,

our eyes on the tree
we can see,
will not see.

Have you ever seen anything so still?
Have you ever seen anything so wild?
I've tried not to murder the child

but the blindness of poetry, I see,
tells me I must. Murder the child, yes, I must.
I shall lay him out in the dust

of a road I remember fifty years ago,
dust that muddied in rain,
vanished in snow,

returned when the sun
did a jig in a ditch
winning all my attention

until I placed my trust
in certain women and men,
dust jigging with dust.

No, I will not murder you.
I'll talk to you, all night.
Your eyes see

the blindness of poetry,
its foolish assaults on silence,
its silence that covers all,

its love of the flesh that is nothing
but a carcase putting on a dress
of rhythms for a blaze of nothingness,

rhythms, rhythms, rhythms in a small room
great as Asia, America, Africa,
offshore islands, great as the name

it strives to put on itself
and cannot. What is the name, I
ask you, what is the name?

Here in the stillness, the wildness,
poetry covers its eyes. Glory? Shame?
It doesn't matter. Whatever it sees

and has seen is slipping away and we
with it. Footsteps, smoke, crows, magpies tell stories.
Out of blind eyes drop mythologies

like tears with a genius for nothing
but whatever tells blind eyes they can see,
dumb voices they can sing,

the blindness of poetry, sweet sad audacious thing,
folly, tyranny, lure beyond all reckoning
insisting always on its right

to make light become dark, dark become light.

Sudden message, instant judgment

The face pushed hotbadbreath into Ace's,
stuck paper into his hand.

'Read this, chum!
Something you know nothing about.
You're not a real poet either.
You have the bourgeois interest at heart!'

The hotbadbreath face scowled off,
smoking.
Papered, Ace stood there, gaping.
Whatever else, he was tops at that.
Gaping.

Strength!

Ace de Horner has a tattoo of Kanooce
on the bicep of his right arm.
'When I look at it,' he mutters to himself
in the Bluebell pad, 'I know I'll never come to harm.

I know I've earned a spot in his pitbull heart
as he is engraved on my skin.
I'm part of him, he of me.
Thank God for the beast within.

When words hack into me like axes
or The Mouth threatens to chew my mind
I caress Kanooce, touch my tattoo.
Amazing what strength I find!'

Strength! That's what Kanooce gives Ace.
Does Ace give anything in return?
If Ace were tattoed on Kanooce's back
would the beast thank God for the man within?

Or would man's image weaken the pitbull heart?
Diminish the hatred that makes him strong
until, if you saw the pair o' them walking the Bluebell way,
you'd wonder which was leading the other along?

Manbeast, beastman, beastmanpoet,
one, all one in sun and rain as it was
in the beginning. Study himthem, as we enter
post-human poetry famined of the primitive-miraculous.

Bubbles

or Janey Mary's *Defense of Poetry*

Janey Mary found Ace making love to Babs
one winter evening in the Bluebell pad.
Janey Mary'd been out shopping
and now she was hopping
mad because there he was, Ace de Horner, astride
Babs, groaning out of him
as if he had some gorgeous pain,
making love to Cleopatra
or Deirdre of the Sorrows
or Marilyn Monroe
or a mechanical compendium of all three.
The old bags was all oh! and ah! and ah! and oh!
   Janey couldn't believe her Liffeybrown eyes.
        She stopped, dumbstruck.
Then she said, 'Fuck you, you randy little rhymer,'
       and pulled him off Babs
who looked neither pleased nor displeased
but stolidly perplexed
         oily
           blue
              pliant
and slightly oversexed.

          Janey Mary grabbed a hammer
and bashed Babs from head to toe,
if that's the way to put it, hard to know
these days. She smashed Babs
again and again till Babs fell apart
at her feet, at her mad heart.
Not bad for a start!
        Then for the first time in her life
Janey Mary grabbed a knife,
turned on Ace in a flash
and cut his willy off. Just like that!
No frills, the willy was off before Ace knew it,
sliced clean as a whistle in Janey Mary's hand.
It was not a remarkable willy
in any sense, just that of your average
Irish poet trying to write poetry with an edge.
Yet it had always done the trick
for Ace and he was quietly proud of it
while at the same time never boasting.

He was glad to know it was there
but didn't publicise the fact
even as he relished the creative act
so penetratingly written about
by generous and snide
bards and critics on either
side of the divide.
      Anyway, there stood Janey Mary with
the poet's johnthomas in her hand, thing of myth
and magic, father of the world, source of
trouble and fun, misery and love
not to mention jokes
of all languages and nations
in all conceiveable situations,
bleeding a little, looking slightly absurd
like an Irishman in exile, poor displaced post-Colonial bird!

Not surprisingly, Ace felt sick.

What is a poet without his prick?
The first draft of Adam? The last Romantic?
How shall he ever reckon the cost
of his paradise lost?

    Out of the Bluebell pad stalked Janey Mary,
off into O'Connell Street, stopped
outside the General Post Office, cocked
her head in the evening crowd
of hard-working martyrs trooping home.
She wanted to proclaim something,
her freedom, independence, refusal to let
a fucking machine make a fool of her
or some pissartist poet muck about with her.
The Dublin air was normal yet sacrificial,
an ageless, grey, palpitating atmosphere
where the stones are fit to howl with laughter.
Well, as the man said, anything can happen here.

      Janey Mary pierced the crowd like a needle
                until she reached
the Floozie in the Jacuzzi. Wild children,
of whom there are thousands astray
both night and day
in this gungho city
(but let them not get in our way)

had flung powder
in the water
and the Floozie was in a state of bubbles,
mad dancing bubbles like the eyes of Dionysos
jigging their lights in the Main Street
of our filthy little metropolis
of muggers druggies robbers vomit piss,
yet terribly beautiful in its way.
Over to the Jacuzzi stepped Janey Mary
and stood a moment on the edge. Then she dropped
the poet's johnthomas into the bubbles
the swirling bobbiting Dionysiac bubbles.

Johnthomas dropped instantly out of sight
like a toppled Taoiseach
or last month's war
or an old star actor compelled to live
a wizened caricature of legendary good looks
or an off-key prophecy sinking through time.
Janey Mary said 'Ah, good night,'
and went for a pint of Guinness
or three. Then she walked back
to the Bluebell pad
where she found Ace in a state
of agony, dazed, disbelieving, fit
to piss himself, if he could.
Well, he did, in a way, but it was
the oddest piss he'd ever had.
He pissed pain and comedy
and comedy is the colour of blood
when it's turning black.
That's what makes people laugh,
funny tears lashing like rain
on the roots of pain.

'Where's my prick?' Ace shouted at Janey Mary.

'The Floozie in the Jacuzzi has it,' she replied,
'and I'd advise you to get down there straightaway
if you wish to recover your little flute.
O my darling poet, you do look cute,
suddenly alive to the art of survival
and rotton-ripe for a revival!'

Ace de Horner rang the police
and told them his story. The squad-car
was at the Jacuzzi in no time
and a young eagle-eyed Gárda from Dublin
destined, years later,
to become Assistant Chief Commissioner
despite sharp competition
from a Roscommon farmer's son
who, touched by the staggering variety of crime,
wrote verse in his spare time,
found the poet's flute under the bubbles,
the wild, rejoicing, voluptuous bubbles.
Paradise lost was cold, limp, offcolour, cleaner
than it had been for years,
since cradled Ace, in fact, rocked to and fro
      warming to his destiny
         like a nappy.

That, like the Golden Age, was long ago.

        Ace was rushed to hospital
where they surgeoned his willy back on
with the patience and skill
it takes to make a poem of the kind
that will animate the blood, stretch the mind
      while reminding the reader
        of how it's possible
he may be blind, he may be blind.

It took a while, several months in fact,
but paradise lost renewed itself mirac-
ulously. The poet lay on his back
and meditated.
           That woman.
Who was Janey Mary?
Was she a demon?
Why had he often thought her an angel?
Was she angel and demon in one?
Was that the woman? How could he know?
If he knew, how could he tell?
Was Janey Mary all he knew
of earth and heaven and hell?

Janey Mary threw Babs in the Liffey
and re-installed Ace in the Bluebell pad.
'You're a bad contraption,' she said, 'a really bad
contraption at times, but I hope you've learned
your lesson.'

'I have,' said Ace 'I have. I'm a changed man.'

'And how's the poet's flute today?' said Janey Mary.

Ace smiled a small, specific smile.

'Fine,' he said. 'Fine. Better than ever. Stronger
and, as God is my judge, longer.'

'I'm delighted to hear that,' said Janey Mary,
'that's a great bit o' news. Isn't it marvellous
what one chop of a knife will do for a man
when he abandons woman for a machine.
One chop of a knife! Good for the poetry too,
I'd say. Kinda forces you to stay true.
Take care of your charlie, love,' she said, 'and make sure
it has a natural future.'

'I'll do that,' said Ace, 'I'm a changed man.
I'll keep an eye on that devil from now on.'

'Good,' said Janey Mary. 'I want to slip out now
to do a bit of shopping.
Just some bubbly stuff for the bath.
Let's have a bath together, shall we, darling,
to celebrate the fact
that once again you're a whole man,
the full shillin', no longer offside.
        A nice bubbly bath
    with my very favourite poet, eh?'

'Good idea,' said Ace, nervously happy.
'Great idea. A bath with Janey Mary.'

'Now you have it,' she smiled. The smile seemed
electricity and God's light, as though
despite this risky scene of touch-and-go
where what is done sometimes touches what is dreamed,
there was an end, it seemed, to all her troubles.
Still smiling, Janey Mary went shopping for bubbles.

Ace de Horner, restored to what
he had been, though for a while was not,
sat,
brooded on the mystery of life:
knife woman machine
        bubbles
            blood
                bubbles
                    machine woman knife.

Never too late to nibble

'My love for you,' he said, 'is stronger
    than anything I saw in the world
        when I had my sight.'

'My love for you,' she chirped, 'is something
        made of recycled
            plastic bottles.
                My coat of love
                    is warm and light
                        this cold night.'

'You're a daft kitten,' he said.

'And you,' she laughed, 'are a blind
        old horse in bed,
    so old, so blind, so horsey
    I think I'll put you out on grass.'

'On grass? Then teach me how to nibble,' pleaded Ace.
'I'll stay alive if I but nibble well.'

'Teach you how to nibble well?
Of course I will, my love, of course I will.
It's never too late to learn another skill.'

'I know, my love, I know.'

'Ready, then, my blind old horse? Here we go.'

Published at last!

Ace stood on O'Connell Bridge, dropped
his poems in the Liffey. One by one
they floated down the air, fell
into the scummy water. One by one
by one they went from him as they had
come to him,
              down the foul air
    into the foul river –

           all he knew of love
           killers he'd met in public
           his education in hate
           stories sharp as
           Janey Mary's words
           dreams nightmares readings
           wisps of hope and horror
           bits and pieces of the city
           that raged and slept in him
           like hell and heaven and the little
           he knew of earth

fell-floated
    down the air
        into the Liffey
           and drifted
             out to sea
                slowly
                    calmly

like happy ghosts.

He never felt stronger in his life.

The slate was clean.

Could be he'd start again.

He knew he still wanted to know how he felt
    about children, women, men

        and pass it on,
the fleshmessage of a skeleton.

Silently, he blessed the poisoned tide
and turned to face

a croak of seagulls heckling

his riverdance race.

Laugh

Beyond all the worlds
   where nothing is seen
      and stars have ended

   Dublin winks

      in the infinite darkness

and down on the town
     and all around
        comes the sound
        of laughter

laughter untrammelled
     laughter of nowhere

abundant
   dancing
      exorcist
        laughter

Brendan Kennelly was born in 1936 in Ballylongford, Co. Kerry, and was educated at St Ita's College, Tarbert, Co. Kerry; at Trinity College, Dublin, where he gained his BA, MA and PhD, and Leeds University. He has lectured in English Literature at Trinity College since 1963, and became its Professor of Modern Literature in 1973. He has also lectured at the University of Antwerp and in America, at Barnard College and Swarthmore College. He has won the AE Memorial Prize for Poetry and the Critics' Special Harveys Award.

He has published more than twenty books of poems, including *My Dark Fathers* (1964), *Collection One: Getting Up Early* (1966), *Good Souls to Survive* (1967), *Dream of a Black Fox* (1968), *Love Cry* (1972), *The Voices* (1973), *Shelley in Dublin* (1974), *A Kind of Trust* (1975), *Islandman* (1977), *A Small Light* (1979) and *The House That Jack Didn't Build* (1982). *The Boats Are Home* (1980) is still available from Gallery Press and *Moloney Up and At It* from the Mercier Press (Cork and Dublin).

He is best-known for two controversial poetry books, *Cromwell*, published in Ireland in 1983 and in Britain by Bloodaxe Books in 1987, and his epic poem *The Book of Judas*, which topped the Irish bestsellers list when it was published by Bloodaxe in 1991. His third epic, *Poetry My Arse* (Bloodaxe Books, 1995), may outdo these in notoriety.

His books of poems translated from the Irish include *A Drinking Cup* (Allen Figgis, 1970) and *Mary* (Aisling Press, Dublin 1987), and his translations are now collected in *Love of Ireland: Poems from the Irish* (Mercier Press, 1989). He has edited several anthologies, including *The Penguin Book of Irish Verse* (1970; 2nd edition 1981), *Between Innocence and Peace: Favourite Poems of Ireland* (Mercier Press, 1993), *Ireland's Women: Writings Past and Present*, with Katie Donovan and A. Norman Jeffares (Gill & Macmillan, 1994), and *Dublines*, with Katie Donovan (Bloodaxe Books, 1995). He has also published two novels, *The Crooked Cross* (1963) and *The Florentines* (1967).

He is also a celebrated dramatist whose plays include versions of *Antigone*, produced at the Peacock Theatre, Dublin, in 1986 (due out from Bloodaxe in 1996); *Medea*, premièred in the Dublin Theatre Festival in 1988, toured in England in 1989 by the Medea Theatre Company, and broadcast by BBC Radio 3 in 1991 (published by Bloodaxe in 1991); *The Trojan Women*, first staged at the Peacock Theatre (published by Bloodaxe in 1993); and Lorca's *Blood Wedding*, to be premièred by Northern Stage in Newcastle (and published by Bloodaxe) in 1996. His stage version of *Cromwell* played to packed houses in Dublin and London. His selection *Landmarks of Irish Drama* was published by Methuen in 1988.

His *Journey into Joy: Selected Prose*, edited by Åke Persson, was published by Bloodaxe in 1994, along with *Dark Fathers into Light*, a critical anthology on his work edited by Richard Pine.

He has published six volumes of selected poems, most recently *A Time for Voices: Selected Poems 1960-1990* (Bloodaxe, 1990) and *Breathing Spaces: Early Poems* (Bloodaxe, 1992).